AF687965

Passive Stock Investing for Beginners

A Comprehensive Guide to Stock Market Investing, Unlocking Financial Success in The Best Way Through Disciplined Passive Investing

By **Brian Scott Fitzgerald**

Published By **Fitzgerald Publishing Group**

© Copyright Fitzgerald Publishing Group 2023 - All rights reserved.

The content contained within this book may not be reproduced, duplicated, or transmitted without direct written permission from the author or the publisher.

Under no circumstances will any blame or legal responsibility be held against the publisher, or author, for any damages, reparation, or monetary loss due to the information contained within this book. Either directly or indirectly. You are responsible for your own choices, actions, and results.

Legal Notice:

This book is copyright protected. This book is only for personal use. You cannot amend, distribute, sell, use, quote, or paraphrase any part of this book's content without the author's or publisher's consent.

Disclaimer Notice:

Please note that the information contained within this document is for educational and entertainment purposes only. All effort has been executed to present accurate, up-to-date, and reliable, complete information. No warranties of any kind are declared or implied. Readers acknowledge that the author does not render legal, financial, medical, or professional advice. The content within this book has been derived from various sources. Please consult a licensed professional before attempting any techniques outlined in this book.

By reading this document, the reader agrees that under no circumstances is the author responsible for any direct or indirect losses incurred because of the use of the information contained within this document, including, but not limited to, — errors, omissions, or inaccuracies.

How to Make Money Online: THE SERIES

I created a series of 12 (twelve) books on How to Make Money Online.

Feel free to read any of my books in the series, which can be found on my Author page on Amazon

You can visit this link or Scan this QR code to get access

https://www.amazon.com/author/brianscottfitzgerald.

Table of Contents

Your Free Gift.

Thank you for your purchase; I'm offering my readers the FREE PDF version of ChatGPT Prompts.

To get almost instant access, go to this website. https://go.fitzgeraldpublishing.com/opt-in-page-passive

Or use your phone to take a picture of this QR code, and it will take you to the Website for your Gift.

Inside the book, you will discover:

- **3000 Prompts** To help you make even more money online.
- **Save time:** You can search for new topics to create content on ChatGPT.
- **Expand knowledge:** Our Package of ChatGPT Prompts covers various topics, from science and technology to art and culture.

If you want to make even more money online, grab this free PDF.

Wait, that's not all; just for buying this book and getting the free PDF above, you can also earn another free Book.

You can use your phone to take a picture of this QR code.

Use the latest AI techniques to uncover online innovation's future. Take advantage! "Beyond ChatGPT and 50 New AI Tools: The Ultimate Guide to Discovering Cutting-Edge AI Tools Beyond ChatGPT" offers endless possibilities. Explore a variety of cutting-edge AI solutions to transform your work. Discover advanced AI tools beyond ChatGPT on this thrilling voyage.

Grab this free book if you want to make even more money online.

Introduction

So, you have, for some reason, decided to invest in the stock market, or at least, you're now thinking about it. Perhaps you heard the success story of someone who invested in the stock market or saw it on TV or elsewhere. Whatever your reasons are (and they are essential), they've led you to this little book to help you get where you want to be.

Investment is a necessary part of life; everybody is investing something into another thing. Investments work on the principle of delayed gratification. In other words, it involves you paying something right now in the hope that it will produce more substantial dividends in the future. For example, a young man that decides to eat healthier is investing in his health. He is settling in the hope that he will reap some benefits in the future, such as a healthier and better life. Thus, we can see that investing is a significant part of life. Why don't most people understand the Stock Market and its workings?

Like any other thing in modern times, the entire system of

Stocks, the stock market, and investments have become so complex that it's easy to feel that you need to be some professional or guru to succeed at investing in the stock market.

Good news, you don't. While the steps and services of an expert in the industry, like a broker or a brokerage, you can still do well-selling stocks as you are. How? That's what this book is about.

I created this fantastic guide for beginners who wish to invest in the stock market but do not know how to go about it. You, like many others, probably do not know much, if anything, about the stock market. You don't know what strategies to use or even what a P/E ratio is. That's why I've put this book in your hands. With a little application and dedication and this excellent little book, you'll understand precisely what the stock market is about, why you should invest in it, and every other thing you'll need to know to become successful at trading stocks.

In this book, I present Stock Trading in straightforward terms; the entire concept of stock and why investing in stocks is sensible. I then show you case studies of those who have spent time trading the stock market, become experts at it, and are wealthy along the way. It doesn't matter why you are approaching the stock market, whether it's to build a nice little nest egg for yourself and your family, increase your family's status, or perhaps you are looking to build capital for your business. Whatever your reason, investing in the stock market makes these dreams possible.

One thing that we will look at quite early is why exactly you are trading. Contrary to many people's opinions, people invest in the stock market for various reasons, and that alone will dictate how your investment should and could be managed. Understanding yourself, your needs, and your goals as you invest helps you set realistic goals and approach the market with the right frame of mind.

Before we even get deep into stock market investing and the strategies you should employ, we'll examine the crucial subject of risk. This is one subject that every participant in the stock market must understand, novice or not. How much trouble are you taking on, and what is the potential reward ratio? If one thing causes problems for stock market investors, it is not managing their risks well. Fortunately, I talk extensively about risks and how to handle them properly. You don't want to be that guy who is too shy and always misses opportunities. At the same time, you do not want to be the guy that jumps on every bandwagon and buys any stocks you can get your hands on until you get into trouble. Just keep this in mind as you go forward.

"High Risk, High Reward, Low risk, Low Reward."

Now, there might be a question in your mind, why should you listen to me? I've been investing in the stock market for years and have profited considerably. I have also been a teacher to countless other people in different situations. I've helped them excel along the journey and even surpass their goals. Of course, with my experience, I realize there is no "one-size-fits-all" approach to help people start with Stock Marketing. Why? Because people are different. Their motivations, learning styles, and thinking patterns all differ.

Hence, you'll have to eventually work on it to get an investment system ideally suited to you. Whatever you think you do or don't know, you'll agree with me that there is a profit to be made by trading stocks. Stocks are an excellent way to increase your profit margins. For example, if you bought $1,000 worth of stock on Netflix in 2007, it will have been worth over $50,000 in 2017. An investment of the same amount in Apple will have netted you about $12,000 within ten years. Yes, these kinds of profits are indeed possible. However, the question is, how do you know the best companies to invest in nowadays? Let me explain a bit further. The whole concept of a stock is to buy a share in a company, then as the company's value increases, your stock grows and becomes more valuable. While this is probably an oversimplification, it's perfect for now. So, the challenge remains, how do you identify the companies of the future? This is because, for a single success story, many companies probably flopped, folded up, and lost value.

However, this book examines how to identify value stocks and killer opportunities and how to take advantage of them. We'll look at exactly how to identify and value stocks and how and what to avoid when trading. We will also look at the investment strategy you must implement to reach your desired goals as soon as possible. Along the journey, we'll examine some of the most excellent stock market investment strategies that some of the best investors have used successfully for years.

Granted, the strategies in this book will take time to make you rich. However, you will learn the essential things, how to keep your money and avoid buying stocks in companies headed for the rocks. In other words, you have my word that by following the strategies and instructions in this book, you will increase your portfolio slowly and steadily, and after looking back in a few years, you'll be shocked at how far you've come. I cannot give you arbitrary numbers and percentages of the profits that you will make. Your success as a stock market investor largely depends on you. Your willingness, determination, and consistency in applying what you've learned will determine how far you'll go as an investor in the stock market. This book is as comprehensive as possible, and as such, I can promise that if you read it, understand, and follow the strategies in this book, you'll learn to avoid the common pitfalls that occur many a stock market investor and well, that makes you much better than any run of the mill investor, and puts you at a higher chance of first NOT losing all your investment and, of course, making a tidy sum of profit from your investments.

Plus, it would be best to understand that you miss out on the wonders of compound interest every day you don't invest in a day. For example, if you invest 7.5% annually, a $10,000 initial investment will grow to $20,000 in 10 years, then $42,000 in the next ten years. After 40 years of steady growth, that $10,000 will have grown into $180,000. Your investment will snowball in the later years because of compound interest. So, investing sooner rather than later is in your best interest. Plus, this is the era of startups. If you can purchase stock in a great company, your profit margin can grow expo-mentally.

Finally, I can say with absolute certainty that the strategies I share in this book are real-life ones that I have used personally, seen others use, and helped others to make an unbelievable amount of returns on the stock market. (Of course, this depends on you putting the work in). Each chapter of the book will outline what you need to do in simple, straightforward, and easy-to-understand language to apply what you've learned to start making a profit. With every chapter you use, you move closer to gaining financial freedom and living your desired life.

Ready? Fasten your seatbelts, open your mind, and come with me on a journey into Stock Market Investing.

CHAPTER ONE

Why You Should Invest In The Stock Market

At some point in your life, you probably will have some money saved and start thinking,. "I probably should invest this into something." You can't live in this modern age and be deaf to the oft-repeated advice of the way that leads to financial freedom.

Save and Invest

That advice is solid. If you are going to be free financially and accessible early, you will have to diversify your income or at least find a way of using money to make more money. Money is simply an asset but a depreciating asset. In other words, due to inflation, your money will lose value steadily and progressively.

Money and Inflation

Here's what I mean. If you dug into the ground, hid $1000 way back in 1960, and then dug it up in 2016, you'd have lost about $7,000. Why? The answer is inflation. Generally, money loses value the longer it is kept. What does this mean for you? It means you'll need more money in the future than you'll need today, even if your expenses do not increase.

The rate at which your money loses value depends on the inflation rate, and since 2000, the inflation rate annually is between 1% and 4%. That means your money loses value by about 1% to 4% annually. This is the issue with many 'safe' investment options. The interest rate will probably earn you enough for your money to retain the same value. In 2018, for instance, the inflation rate in the United States was 2.4%, and the best 'safe' investment you'd probably have found online was a 6-year CD from a commercial bank, offering 2.7% per year. Plus, there's no assurance that the inflation rate wouldn't have increased to 3% or even more. If you've saved up enough money to buy a Toyota, then keep the money under your mattress for about 20 or 30 years, then when you.

Take it out. It'll probably be enough to buy a bicycle. Invest it with your local bank In a Certificate of Deposit, and then, in 30 years, it'll still be able to buy you a Toyota. Invest in the stock market, however, and you can probably get a Maserati or something fancier. That is why investing is a no-brainer. While saving is a good strategy for managing your money in the short term, you need a plan for investing for a long time.

Why You Should Save

Ok, I know you've seen this everywhere. Everybody, at one time or the other, has been asked to save. If you are reading a book on the stock market and how to get into it, you probably already have a saving habit, or if you don't, you at least know why you should save.

Saving is a good strategy for anybody. No matter who you are, what you do, or how much you earn, saving a percentage of whatever you make is good practice. Many systems have been proposed, from keeping the biblical tithe to an 80-10-10 model. You spend 80% of what you earn, use 10% to pay off debts, or give to charity, whichever works for you, and save the final 10%. There are other versions of these systems, including some ruthless ones. I remember reading somewhere that you should save 60% of your income. Hey, whatever floats your boat!

My primary concern, however, isn't that you should save; instead, it is on what you do with that money. Depending on how much you earn and your responsibilities, you can have $1000 and more saved up per annum. The thing is, as good as savings are, they are still dependent on active income. You can only save from what you earn, and if you only save money for a long time, eventually, you will stop working, then what happens then? That is why I believe in investments and the power of interest. In other words, don't stop at setting some money aside. While it is a good idea, saving and storing it will eventually make it useless if you don't invest it.

Did you need more convincing? Let's look at something the great Albert Einstein described as the 8th wonder of the world and how it applies to your money.

The Wonders of Compound Interest

The stock market is an excellent place to invest your Money. You could make a tidy sum if you take it slow and steady and invest intelligently. The wonders of stock market investing become apparent when you do a little math with compound interest. What is compound interest? It is interest that is added to the claim that you already have.

Let me break it down for you. In the case of simple Interest, if you invest $1000, and the interest rate is 10% per annum, then the same interest will be the same yearly. That means that in the first year, you'll get interest of $100, the same in the second year and the same in the third year, and so on. At the end of 5 years, you'll have $1,500 as your investments + interest. With compound interest, however, at the end of the first year, you'll get $100 as interest, with $1,100 after the first year. In the second year, however, the 10% interest is calculated on the $1100 that you now have, so the interest of the 2nd year will now be 10% of $1100, giving you the interest of $110, so the total you get at the end of the 2nd year is $1,210. You do the same for the 3rd year, the 4th, the 5th, and so on. At the end of the 5th year, you'd have $1,610.51 as your investment + interest.

I know this probably looks small, but let's consider another scenario. If you have $10,000 saved up and then invest it at a rate of 7%, which is an average gain rate for investments in the stock market, then you will have $20,000 in 10 years. That means you'll ignore your original $10,000 and another $10,000 you made from investing. What's better, this is passive income. You don't need to leave your job to be able to get it. Instead, it grows and matures independently (of course, provided you did your homework well and invested smartly).

The incredible power of compound interest made Albert Einstein call it the world's eighth wonder. He famously said compound interest was the "eighth wonder of the world, and that he under- stands it earns, and he that doesn't pay for it." Compound interest does not seem like much when you start small, but leave it to accumulate over time, and you'll be amazed at how lucrative it can be.

Investing in the stock market helps you tap into this incredible power. Going by our earlier example, if you are a prudent saver and can save up to $10,000 per year and then invest it into the stock market every year, you can do that for 30 years. You will have invested $300,000 in the market. If you invested smartly, didn't take too many risks, and the world didn't end, then at the end of that 30 years, guess how much you'll have received as profit? A whopping $710,730. In other words, in 30 years, an investment of $10,000 per year will be worth over a million dollars. If the stock market can help ordinary people become financially free, why don't more people invest in it?

What You Need to Know About the Stock Market

In the late 1990s, investment was the new craze; everybody was investing in something, whether established companies, .com businesses, or real estate. Estimates say that about 50% of Americans invested in one thing or another around this time. However, many investors became wary of investing with the crash of the .com bubble in the early 2000s, the real estate crises in 2000, and the stock market crash in 2008. Just do a Google search of "Should I invest in stocks" and see an overwhelming number of results that tell you no. While it is true that the stock market may not be everything, I genuinely believe that anybody can invest and make money from it if they are willing to do the work. Throughout these crashes, many investors have realized they must become knowledgeable about their investment instead of leaving it to the "so-called experts." It makes no sense to me that you will invest your hard-earned money in a business without learning about what you are investing in and how the market works. Granted, you will not become an expert broker, but with the abundance of knowledge available today, you owe it to yourself and your future to learn about the stock market and how it works. I'm not talking about going to study to become a broker; instead, I'm talking about giving your attention and time to material like this book you are reading to attending investment meetups so that you can become a more confident investor. Historically, stocks have earned more than any other form of investment for their investors. According to the records, investors in the US Profited the most by buying stocks than any different kind of investment option.

Another advantage of investing in the stock market is its simplicity. With the advent of the Internet, you can trade remotely and buy stock from a broker with a few clicks. Of course, you should ensure that you do market research on each store that you buy from. Remember, you must be able to learn to understand the stock market, how it works, and how to profit from it.

Stock Market Strategies

In this book, you'll not see many rules; instead, you'll find it full of case studies, suggestions, and explanations. That is because there is no real hard and fast rule to how you invest. There are simply some basic principles that you need to follow, as well as some background information that will serve you well. Generally, however, in my years of investing and helping others invest in stocks, here are some basic lessons that I've learned.

Buy Stocks when they are rising in price rather than falling. And when buying more stocks, you should only buy them when the price has risen higher than the original purchase price, not when it drops below it. You should purchase supplies when they are nearer to the annual high. Don't buy when the stock has sunk so low that it looks cheap. It would help if you purchased relatively higher-priced stocks than lower-priced ones. Also, learn to sell stocks with a little loss rather than just waiting to recoup losses with the stock bouncing back. Maybe taking this loss is the best gain you can make for your overall percentage gain in inventories.

When studying the companies that you want to invest in, you should pay less attention to the book value, dividends, and PE ratios (don't worry, we'll cover all these shortly) – The last 100 years have shown that they aren't as indicative of progress s they sound.·These indices do not point to America's most successful businesses. Instead, it would help if you focused on factors that have reliably been shown to reflect the real success of a company, such as the rate of profit growth, the price, and volume action. You should also consider if the company is a profit leader in its industry and how superior its products are.

While analysis and breakdowns from "experts" are valuable, you don't want to base your entire investment strategy on them. Don't allow these reports and recommendations to influence you overly. After all, analysts wrote them who are expressing their opinions could very well be wrong. Lastly, make charts your best friend. Numbers never lie, and if you're going to be successful as an investor, you must be able to read and interpret the information provided by graphs. Coincidentally, all these actions run contrary to our fundamental human nature. We love to jump on the bandwagon when things are going well and jump off when things aren't. The reality is that the stock market, like any other market, is simply a theatre where human nature and crowd psychology are put on display. The laws of supply and demand also play a part here too.

A study of the chart patterns today reflects the same things they did 50 or even 100 years ago. Although the players have changed, the game and the rule haven't. Understanding the principles that have driven the stock market's success for 100s of years will allow you to build up your portfolio and invest smartly and sensibly to build a great future. By studying the chart patterns of the stock market success stories, you can identify better stocks and companies to invest in and help you run far away from the ones that look promising but are doomed for failure.

Voices in the Market

There are a million and one voices in the market today in the form of books, research papers, expert websites, and blogs that seemingly have the "best" advice on investing in the stock market. The direction can sometimes be opposite and yet be proven to have worked for proponents of each strategy. My aim isn't to be another voice in the market but to show you a way.

Remember, I assume you are holding this book and don't know Jack about the stock market or investing in it, so I wrote this book to give your insight into the world of stocks. Also, I will explain some of the basic principles that guide the stock market and then describe with case studies what strategies have worked and why they did. As you read this book, you will find among these strategies the one that suits you the best and allows you to express yourself in the best way. There are many paths to success here, and my job is not to sell you my course but to show you how to find your path.

As I stated earlier, there isn't a one-size-fits-all approach to investing; only one way is the best for you and how to find it.

The Rock Stars of Investments

Stock market investors come in many shapes and sizes, but some prolific individuals have made extraordinary success by investing. The most exciting thing is that many of these industry leaders have varying views on approaching the market, yet all succeeded as investors. Success in investing is not about the path taken but the journey itself. Let's look at some success stories from investors and see what they have to say. And if you haven't done so yet, find books, blogs, or any articles written by these folks, as it will help you make even more money in Stocks.

Ben Graham

Ben Graham was a successful investment manager and an excellent finance teacher. Among his contribution to the industry were two classics on investments still in use today. He is also recognized for fathering two fundamental disciplines in acquisition – value investing and security analysis.

The essence of value investing is that any single investment must be worth substantially more than the investor must pay. He was an ardent believer in fundamental analysis. He consistently invested in companies that had solid balance sheets or companies with little to no debts, profit margins that were above average, and healthy cash flow.

John Templeton

He was one of the 20th-century contrarians and was said he "bought low in the Depression, sold high during the Internet boom, and made many good calls in between." He created some of the world's most significant and successful investment funds internationally. He later sold his Templeton funds to Franklin Group in 1992. In 1999, Money Magazine described him as "*arguably the greatest stock picker of the century.*" He was eventually knighted for his many accomplishments.

Thomas Rowe Price, Jr.

He is considered the father of "growth investing." He was formed in the struggle with the Depression, and he learned not to stay out of stocks but, instead, to embrace them. He was a crowd-opposer, with views contrary to his days. In his opinion, he saw financial markets as operating on a cycle and believed in investing long-term in good companies. While this is a popular opinion today, it was virtually unheard of in his days. His philosophy was that investors should focus on picking individual stocks on a long-term basis. He rose to success on the wings of discipline, consistency, process, and fundamental research.

John Neff

John joined Wellington Management Co. in 1964 and stayed with them for over 30 years, managing 3 of their funds then. He preferred to invest in industries that were popular via indirect paths. Neff was considered a value investor, as he focused on companies with low P/E ratios and high dividends yielded. He also managed the Windsor Fund for over 30 years, which ended in 1995, with a record return of 13.7%, more significant than the S&P 500 for that same period. In other words, the fund made a gain of 55 times the initial investment made in 1964.

Jesse Livermore

Livermore needed formal training in stock trading or even formal education. He was a trader who learned from both his wins and losses. Many successes and failures cemented the trading ideas you can still find today. He began trading early, in his teenage years, and by fifteen, had reportedly produced profits of $1,000 and above, which was serious money in his days.

Peter Lynch

He managed the Fidelity Magellan Fund from 1977 to 1990, in which their assets skyrocketed to $14 billion from $20 million.

More importantly, it was recorded that Lynch repeatedly beat the S&P 500 index benchmark for 11 of those 13 years, with an average return of 29% annually.

He was often described as a chameleon who adapted to whatever investment style worked at that time. However, when picking specific stocks, he stuck to what he knew or could readily understand.

Warren Buffet

Last on the list is the Oracle of Omaha. He is considered one of the most successful investors in the history of investing. A follower of Benjamin Graham's principles, he built a multi-billion-dollar fortune mainly by buying stocks and companies through Berkshire Hathaway. To compare his success, an investment of $10,000 in Berkshire Hathaway in 1965 will be worth more than $50 million today. Buffet's investing style is disciplined, patient, and value driven. All traits that have seen him outperform the market and emerge as one of the wealthiest men in the world.

Now that we've looked at a few successes, you can see that their success wasn't tied to a single strategy. Instead, their understanding of the market, patience, and commitment to a process that worked for them made all the difference. And as you step out into the world of stock market investing, doing the same will make and keep you successful.

Chapter Two

The Fundamentals To Understand

In straightforward terms, investment is laying out money now with the expectation of receiving more money in the future. At Berkshire, it was more comprehensively described as forgoing consumption now to have the ability to consume more later. Investment is, in other words, a consideration of tomorrow while living today. It is like the agricultural concept of sowing in winter and reaping in summer or the proverbial idea of "making hay while the sun shines." You invest in your hay days to enjoy your gray years better. It is a means to a successful and fruitful end. Here, you will learn that:

- Investment is committing money somewhere, hoping for a later return or profit.
- Unlike instant resource consumption, it sets money aside for the future to grow.
- It is a life risk, and it is a probable loss.
- Stock market investment offers the best investment

experience to beginners.

As investors, we will learn how to maximize returns and profits while minimizing costs and possible losses.

What is the Nature of your Investment?

Before opening any online broker like Fidelity, etc., somebody will question you on the kind of investment you are open to and the level of risk you can take, hence the question; what kind of investor are you? Before you give your money away, you must answer these questions because it will translate to the value of your money.

Some individual investors are open to putting the money out there in the spirit of "I hope it comes out good," while others are up to track and follow up on the progress of their investment. **Online Brokers**

There are full-service brokers and discount brokers. The former provides exclusive financial advisory services on various sectors of their investor's lives, they charge significantly as a result, and the high-net-worth owners populate their clients. While discount brokers provide tools for picking your transaction choice, most advocate the set-in-and-forget-it offer. Subsequently, online brokers have updated their services in this century with educative resources on the Internet and mobile apps. Though some brokers are without deposit restrictions, investors might be challenged with other limitations and charges to the unlimited deposit accounts. Before investing, one must keep this in mind.

Robo-advisor:

The goal is to utilize technology to reduce investor costs and streamline investment advice. The robot advisor resulted after the 2008 crisis in finance. *Betterment* is often reputed to be the first; after its launch, other robot companies have come up, like *Charles Schwab*. If you want an algorithm to evaluate and make decisions for your investment, including tax-loss investment and rebalancing, that is what the robot advisor was made for. A long-term wealth builder or an intending long-term investor will need it for investment analysis.

Investing Via Your Employer

For someone on a tight budget or a not so high- income earner, invest as low as 1% of your income through your employer. This is deducted before taxes are, straight from your paycheck. A 1% into your retirement plan will likely not hurt so much, and subsequently, with adaptation and management, you could increase the percentage and add up your investment.

Minimum Amount to Create an Account

Most institutes offering financial services have a minimum level for deposits. Some companies might not even proceed with your application with less than $1,000 readily available for a warranty. You can cross-check for the best viable option to suit your budget plan. And you should view and examine the brokers' reviews. Some firms do not require a minimum deposit amount; others have lower management and trading fees costs, while others might offer free commissions on specific terms and conditions.

Commissions and Fees

Economically, trades are on give and take, and nothing goes for nothing. Everything comes with a price. Some brokers might be racing to provide little or no commissions, but they are not charity organizations and must make it by other means. With low commissions on trade for investors, which incentivizes existing and potential investors, the brokers still must make it up.

Majorly, brokers give charges for trading stocks, the fees ranging from as low as 2% to 10%. While 2% might look like a minute amount, your profitability depends on your trading frequency and investment amount.

For instance, if you have a $2,000 investment and want to buy five different stocks, they are viewed as various trades and charged individually. The fee is 2%, which will make up 10%. On purchasing the five stocks. Your $2000 will be short of $200 already, leaving you with an amount of $1800.

If you decide to sell these stocks again since that is what investment is all about, you will lose the same amount, and in the end, you are at a 20% loss from your initial investment amount just by buying and selling stocks. If you intend to be a frequent stock trader, check the cost-friendly brokers before investing.

Mutual Funds Load (Fees)

Apart from the fees of buying mutual funds, there are other charges to be incurred, including the Management Expenses Ratio (MER), which is charged by the management team and ranges from 0.05% to 0.7% annually. It is diverse according to the funds involved. Fortunately, a high MER earns an equally high investment charge.

In mutual funds purchases, several sales charges are termed "loads": front-end, no-end, and back-end loads. These deserve extra checks to avoid future unexplained additional charges. For beginner investors, mutual fund fees are an advantage because all you need to do is meet the requirements of owning an account, and you can invest as low as $50 monthly in a mutual fund. This is known as Dollar Cost Averaging (DCA).

Reducing Risks by Diversifying

Diversifying means separating your investments to avoid a crash. It is wise not to put your eggs in one basket. Investing in several assets cannot all fail simultaneously, allowing you to stay on top of your game instead of losing it all when one investment fails.

However, as earlier discussed, this has a downturn in trading fees and losses, so for a not-so-large investment fund, you should start up with just two companies at most. Mutual funds and ETFs tend to have more diverse companies and assets within them, making it easy to diversify, and this is an advantage for their investors.

As a beginner investor, you must.

- Be up to date with your limitations and available restrictions.
- Find out the minimum deposit restrictions available and compare commissions.
- Then, the choice of which broker to engage in business with is yours.

What are Stock Fundamentals?

Frequently on investment shows and talks, analysts, executives, fund managers, and investors alike use the word "fundamentals" or about which stock has solid fundamentals and how to build strong fundamentals. Well, opinions vary as others think it needs to be emphasized and more critical. However, what are "fundamentals"?

They are a critical analysis of data, charts, and other terms apart from the primarily focused trading patterns, which may improve the value of the stock. It is technically starting from the basics of the store to build up exceptional value.

It is aimed at a company image, identifying the fundamental value of shares, purchasing based on the information, and so on, as opposed to the "technical analysis," which is all about trading, prices, history, and records. The following are pointers to access the fundamentals of a company:

- Cash Flow
- Assets Return
- Conservative Gearing
- History of Retaining Profits for Future Funding
- Capital Management Soundness for Maximization of Profit and Returns.

Think of a stock market as a trading mall with various goods in diverse categories. Suppose the consumption rate (as in purchase) of gadgets inflates, and the consumers seem to be headed for all the Huawei gadgets. In that case, this will be picked up by a technical analyst and a fundamental analyst. A technical analyst will move with the crowd and aid the purchase by making Huawei gadgets available in surplus, hoping for an increase in price due to demand-pull inflation. However, a fundamental analyst is more profound and product-oriented than a customer-oriented one.

As far as they are concerned, customers are emotionally expressive individuals who cannot be trusted for a balance regarding the actual value of products. The fundamentalists wait for the crowd to clear and then give a situational analysis of the gadgets' scrap value, internal ware, and hardware. This is like an evaluation of value, like a book review. They will focus on the quality of the Huawei gadgets, their functions, portability, battery durability, processor speed, storage capacity, and every other target for value to get the customer's review.

Ultimately, he comes up with an intrinsic value of the gadget that is not dependent on the current price. If the sale price is worth their inherent value, they move on to purchase and, if otherwise, not. Fundamentals with a good deal do not equal profit. It takes work to be a fundamental analyst taking time to evaluate a company's intrinsic value and long-term returns. But this can save an investor the trouble of loss or future uncertainties and fluctuations in investment. A total view of a company does not translate to profit in the long run because investors may run out of luck with delays when the market tides fall. So, investors must be assertive in their investments and investment inquiries.

For a confident investment, there is much that the investor can do to learn and train on the fundamental analysis to identify a stock with solid fundamentals, and they become better stock pickers.

Major Stock Market Terminologies

The stock market is a significant advantage associated with a free market economy by providing stocks, shares, and corporate bonds for individuals to buy. It engages regular investors in sharing companies' profits, earning returns, and making profits through capital gains and dividends, although the risk of losses is not eliminated. These are achieved in many financial ways and services made available.

Price to Earnings Ratio:

This is the ratio of share prices over the annual net income of the firm per each of the shares. It is like the cost of producing a jar of milk relative to the revenue or profit made from the production. A high rate of Price to Earnings Ratio (P.E ratio) indicates increased demand for the product. And otherwise. This ratio is calculated in the number of years to earn enough to pay back the original purchase price. It could also be estimated with proposed estimations of the following year's earnings per share in the denominator. The simple formula is; Price/Earnings per share (EPS) =Price to Earnings Ratio (P.E ratio).

Price to Sales Ratio

This is derived by dividing the per-share stock price by the per-share revenue. It is a metric for valuing stocks and how much investors are willing to pay per dollar for a store, and it is usually done over a Trailing Twelve Months (TTM). Price Sales ratio is most helpful in comparing similar sectors because of industry variance. It is also mainly used for nonprofit organizations because of the limitations that sales may only sometimes reveal the complete picture. Price Sales ratio compares a company's stock price to its revenue over time.

Book Value

This would be the accumulative worth of a company in cash if somebody liquidated its assets with every liability paid for. It is merely the value left of a company after its liabilities and depreciation have been deducted.

Formula: total assets - intangible assets - liabilities = Book value. Deriving a company's book value is nothing tactical, as it is already present in the balance sheets and as "shareholder's equity." For example, if the balance sheets for Cadbury Limited report $365 million as total assets and about $285 million worth of liability, the book value (shareholder's equity) is $80 million.

Meanwhile, Market Value - or Market Cap - refers to the price a company is worth or rated in the market. It is the total value of a company translated into dollar amounts. It is calculated in the units of Current Market Price (CMP). Formula; Market value= company's outstanding shares - CMP.

Book value is significant because, as the intrinsic net value of the company, it serves as a tool for the investors to decide if a company is over or underpriced.

Why Should I Invest?

Individuals who do not invest have no financial life support. You are on eat-as-you-earn, which is much riskier than it is with the risk of loss while investing. Here are reasons why you should invest your money and assets.

- **Money Growth:** investment wagons like stocks, bonds, and deposit certificates offer returns for your investment, which increases your money and allows a gradual build. It aids wealth and asset creation and growth.

- **Save for Retirement:** as I said earlier, investment is living minimally today to have plenty tomorrow. It is wise to save while you work, make your savings into investments like real estate businesses, stocks, bonds, and mutual funds, and at retirement, when there are no longer any steady earnings, you can comfortably live off your life savings and investment. At a young age, one is prone to taking risks; the lower the chances, the better. However, the risk is less when you are young because it's easy to learn from experience, and you have more time to invest. So now is the time to invest.

- **Attainment of financial goals:** Investment aids the achievement of big dreams at a faster rate. Because the interest is more in value and speed than just savings accounts, these investments, when matured, can be used to pursue big dreams like purchasing a big house, a lake house, a business startup, and other seen, foreseen, and unforeseen goals.

- **Increased returns:** As discussed earlier, for a high return, you need to invest in a high place that can offer high returns. You must invest big to save big and get equally significant returns.

- **A chance to get employer's matching programs:** Employers sometimes put it out there for those who invest in a 401k plan to help them top their savings up to a certain amount. And one must meet the stated amount to qualify for this matching.

- **Support others:** Most investors like to invest in people. Apart from the value of land, which does not diminish, next to it is human value. So, investing in humans and being a support system might take time, but it makes such people satisfied and content. However, long-term support means investing rather than living now and paying later.

- **Beating inflation:** It is a known fact that investors gain during inflation. Instead of spending the money you earn just as it comes or trying to save by stuffing your pillows and mattresses, making investments in bonds, buying shares, and so on, prove productive in times of economic instability like inflation.

- **Employing your money:** Most people - if not all - are employed for the salary and financial benefits they hope to get, and they work hard for the latter. Meanwhile, as an investor, you make money work for you and make a twist to the general rules. You invest your money, and without hard work, your money grows, and yields increase. For instance, if I invest as little as $50 at an annual interest rate of 7% over the next 30 years, in the end, I will have made over $350 without lifting a finger.

CHAPTER THREE

How To Get Started Buying And Selling Stocks (And Save On (Fees)

You know the legal term of arbitration, where one guy serves as a medium between two conflicting parties. The arbitrator is not a party to any side but a neutral person who stands in the middle-level ground to resolve a conflict for a price or an agreed pay from both parties. This is different from litigation, where each party has an advocate who stands in defense. The arbitrator is the BROKER, driving this analogy down to the stocks and investments business world, while the litigation advocate can be an AGENT. And they are not the same because one is neutral, whereas the latter must be either white or black and in support of their employer. However, our discussion is targeted at BROKERS. According to Wikipedia, a broker is a person or firm who arranges transactions between a buyer and a seller for a commission when the deal is executed. A broker who acts as a buyer or seller will be referred to as a 'principal' party to the agreement. Brokers, in a nutshell, are the individuals or firms who stage for purchase between two willing parties, and, in the end, they get their cut or percentage profit from the transaction based on the initially agreed rate or mode of payment.

Brokerage Fees

This is the amount a broker gets for successfully staging a purchase. It is the compensation a broker receives as a reward from any transaction, usually based on the value of a percentage of the transaction price.

Workability of Brokerage Fees

Take, for instance, Rowland, an entrepreneur who wants to purchase 250 shares in the ADX group of companies at the rate of $50 per share. Whereas the brokerage rate is at 2%, the cost of the transaction will result in;

250 × $30 = $7500.

$7500 × .02 = $150.

$7500 + $150 = 7650.

After a while, you might resell the shares, which will require the same brokerage fee except if otherwise stated or agreed upon. And at this rate, the investor's transaction will be primarily affected in terms of returns and initial value. The investor will run at a loss, especially with frequent buying and reselling of stocks (changing positions) that only require a little capital. Also, some brokerage firms will charge maintenance and other fees, increasing investor expenses. Knowing the result and making decisions accordingly would help if you made yourself aware of these charges.

However, the deal of brokerage fees depends on the type of broker you invest in. Some full-service brokers provide everything, including trading information, research materials, etc. In contrast, Discount brokers concentrate on the former is more expensive to execute the trade and hardly anything else. The fees go further to gain on the investment size, the number and size of businesses, and the customer's account.

Investors need to evaluate their preferences and the fee structure before choosing a broker to deal with, to avoid a broker that significantly upsets the investor's plan to save money. There are many brokers, so finding a suitable one for your preferred plan should not be difficult.

Best Online Brokers

Online Brokers give you viable access to investment products and packages like bonds, mutual funds, stocks, and ETFs straight out of your mobile smartphone or devices. With the various kinds and brands of brokers online, finding the best might be challenging. Still, according to Investopedia, the brokerages shown below are the best brokers to use based on information collected through user reviews.

- Fidelity Investment
- TD Ameritrade
- Charles Schwab
- Interactive traders
- E*Trade

We will describe them here, showing the pros and cons.

Fidelity Investment:

They offer tools, services, and value, whereas updates and upgrading are ongoing.

Pros:

- Improvement for stock and options trade
- Access to active Trade Pro for all customers
- Low and comprehensive fees

Cons;

- Multiple platforms are needed to access all of their tools.

- The account operation is restricted to only.
- U.S. citizens and residents.

TD Ameritrade:

Pros;

- Availability of exclusive tools and materials
- Novice investors are made comfortable with the educational material offered.
- Channels have been made like, Facebook, Twitter, and so on.

Cons;

- Difficulty in researching because of too much content in the system.
- Multiple trading systems to find the necessary tools

Charles Schwab:

They offer complete services and technology to everyone, that is, self-skilled traders and financial guidance seekers. They also provide full banking capacities and, thus, many other exclusive platforms.

Pros;

- Refund for unhappy or unsatisfied customers

- Mobile web platforms and native mobile apps for functionality.

Cons

- It takes effort to achieve the most desirable features.
- Push towards using financial advisors, which may make them lose confidence in their abilities.

Interactive brokers:

Pros;

- Prices are on the low end.
- A gearing platform for highly active traders
- Excellent analysis features.

Cons:

- Small accounts are subject to fees.
- Education is only offered if they support education accounts.

E* Trade:

Pros;

- Streaming strategy options

- Availability of tools to future traders
- Use of performance risk tools

Cons;

- High level of margin rates
- There is no bank integration.
- There are other listed best brokers, which include:

Robinhood: This broker is best known for the free trade of stocks, unlimited and permanent. It gives access to free options trade and cryptocurrency trades.

Ally Invest: This low-cost brokerage attracts bulk discounts with more trades. It was formerly known as Traducing until 2016. Ally purchased it, and it is beginner friendly. It gives competitive standard pricing even in foreign currencies.

Merrill Edge: this brokerage is taken from Merrill Lynch, a street powerhouse that failed and got sold out in 2008 to the Bank of America. Its primary unique feature is the involvement with the Bank of America rewards program, so for a customer of Bank of America, it is perfect for complying with that account. These brokers have diverse brokerage fees, values, and individual uniqueness, which an investor should consider more carefully while picking any of them, as evaluating available value and preference is necessary when considering investing.

Considerations for Choosing an Online Broker

As a potential investor, you must think and evaluate your needs at that moment and in the most immediate future. Are you a beginner? If so, are you interested in a direct investment or one with educational materials? What is your budget amount for investment? What brokers offer an unlimited deposit for investments? Are you always on the go and a fundamental Internet user? What brokers have incredible mobile apps? How accessible and reliable are the apps on the go?

Going further, you must inquire about yourself and distinguish between "investing and trading" and which interests you. Investing involves taking a sum of money and dumping it somewhere, hoping it will be fertile and grow into long-term assets. Investing is what you do to save for the luxury of the future from right now instead of low-interest rates from mere bank savings accounts. Meanwhile, trading is the buying and selling of assets within a time frame. Trading is short-term and riskier than investment, which is long-term.

These questions must be examined and answered before investing with an online broker. Trade or invest? Accessible mobile app? What sectors to support or trade-in? While asking these questions is essential, getting practical and efficient answers is difficult. However, there are guides to help with the process.

Choosing the Best Online Broker

The following factors will aid you in the evaluation of a broker.

Commissions

Examine the commission on your most feasible option: there are several options for investment, like bonds, mutual funds, ETFs, etc. Some brokers also offer future trading opportunities.

The investment options the broker offers will set the value for commissions and your subsequent satisfaction. The proposals and their incurred commissions are discussed below:

Individual stocks: while charges are still being attached to the buying and selling of stocks by some brokers, there are a few of them available without commissions; E-Trade, Interactive brokers, etc.

Mutual funds: you can limit mutual funds' transaction costs by purchasing from a company with no-transaction-fee mutual funds. Mutual funds attract an internal fee called "expense ratio," which is charged directly by the funds, not the broker.

ETFs are usually purchased for a price just like shares, making them open to the Broker's stock commission. You could get brokers who offer free commission too.

Account Minimums

While some brokers offer limited accounts, mini - mums, others offer unlimited minimum levels, such as Merrill Edge, Ally Vest, and co.

Account Fees

There is no way to shy away from account fees, but you can minimize them. While some brokers will charge you considerably when transferring to a new broker, the new company sometimes offers reimbursement of your fees through limit bonds.

The annual fees, inactivity fees, trading platform sub, and extra charges are widespread charges, and you can easily boycott any additional charges by not choosing the broker that demands them.

Trade techniques and tech needs

As a beginner investor, you may want a helping hand through your learning and informational videos, tutorials, etc. Depending on the broker, these could be offered free to the investors, but the educational offers are primarily made available to all beginner investors.

Utilize Promotions

Promotions are a better reason to invest in a broker. Still, it could spur a choice between picking one that offers enticing offers to the customer, cash bonuses, and deposit amounts and another that does not.

CHAPTER FOUR

Structures To Manage Your Money

This chapter will look at managing your money, primarily via external structures. We'll discuss Money Managers, Financial Advisors, and Mutual Funds. We'll examine if you need them, and how to decide to choose them. Let's get started, shall we?

As we stated at the beginning of this book, the material in this book was written for people with little to no professional or corporate financial management knowledge who want to invest in the Stock Market, and in the previous chapters, we've examined many of the basics that you will need to know to start to play in the world of stocks and investments. But then, the question arises, should you hire a professional financial adviser to help manage your portfolio and investment?

First, it's important to mention that many people realize they cannot solely depend on a financial advisor to manage their portfolios. The crashing of stocks and other markets in recent years has established the need for anyone investing in any market to research and ensure that they gain knowledge in that area. In other words, whether you hire a financial adviser, you cannot afford to slack off learning about the stock market and researching any stock you buy. After all, it makes no sense to trust someone else with your money when you have no idea what they are planning to do with it.

Choosing or Using a Financial Advisor

A financial advisor is someone that helps you manage your money. They allow you to manage investing, saving, and spending money. A financial advisor usually offers a wide range of services on everything related to money. Now, the level of influence and interaction that the financial advisor has with your funds is up to you and the structure between both parties, that is, you and the advisor. Financial advisor covers many services, including investment planning, financial consulting, and certified financial planners. There are also digital financial management options, such as robot advisors, where you are not necessarily interacting with a human manager. But more on this later.

What can a Financial Advisor do for you?

A financial advisor is an expert in financial matters who provides various services to manage money, investments, and savings. Therein lies the core of financial advising. The influence of technology has made it possible for ordinary people to enter the financial market without formal training. That said, certain kinds of knowledge are available to only those formally trained financially and can access and take advantage of them. In other words, the fact that you can access the stock market in some form and make trades means that you know only some things there is to know about the market. This is where a financial advisor comes in.

A financial advisor can, among many other things, help you assess your financial situation, review your financial goals, and help you chart a path to achieve those goals. So, a financial advisor will examine your assets, expenses, and debts and help you identify how exactly you can improve. They can also help you work to reduce spending, figure out insurance and tax, increase your savings, and invest your money. Since financial advisor has professional expertise and experience, they can significantly help you improve your portfolio. A good financial advisor can be of help when it comes to achieving your goals of financial independence and freedom.

Types of Financial Advisors

There are several types of financial advisors, both in terms of the services offered and the contexts in which the services are provided. Let's look at some of these financial advisors:

CFP: A CFP or Certified Financial Planner helps you do just that, plan your finances. A professional board in your country must issue a license in your country, such as the Certified Financial Planning Board of Standards in the U.S. To become a CFP, people must educate themselves thoroughly, pass a rigorous test, and demonstrate work experience.

These kinds of financial advisors are primarily aimed at helping you create actionable goals for your finances that you should follow to achieve your plan as you go on.

Broker/Stockbroker: This financial advisor assists you with investments and explains how to invest your money. A stockbroker buys or sells financial products (i.e., stocks) for their customers and typically receives a fee for doing this. To become a broker, you must be licensed by the U.S. Security and Exchanges Commission in the US or any other equivalent board in any country where you may be based.

A Registered Investment Advisor: This advisor gives investors advice and recommendations. RIAs are usually registered with the Security and Exchange Commission or some other form of investor, depending on the company's size or size. Some Investment advisors focus on investment portfolios, while others take a more general and holistic view.

Also, it is not uncommon for a particular individual or company to offer the services of more than just one specific discipline. The reason for this is that it is not. It is very realistic for an average person to employ a CFP only to plan their finances and simultaneously hire another broker to solely manage financial instruments and other investments. Many individual economic advisors are licensed to act in multiple offices, or the company they work for offers these services as part of a particular package.

How much does it cost to hire a Financial Advisor?

Perhaps you are already thinking, if a financial advisor is this good, or can offer this level of services, then I should patronize them; well, pump your brakes first. It would help to consider the cost implications of hiring a financial advisor. Many advisors charge different fees at different rates, but here are some more common ones.

Hourly Rates: Some advisors charge between $75 and $350 per hour. The average rates tend to hover around $150.

Set Fees: Some Financial advisors also request a fixed fee for performing a specific work. It could range from a couple hundred to even thousand dollars.

Monthly Fees: This option is usually reserved for those planning to use the advisor or their company's services for a long time. The advisor and the client can work out a specific fee that someone will pay monthly if you utilize their services. The price could also be a portion of the money you sought to invest.

Manage an Ongoing Fee: This scenario is closely related to paying a monthly fee for an ongoing service. These are some of the combinations of fees that financial advisors can charge, and as you can see, they are expensive. Imagine that you must pay a monthly service fee or a percentage of your investment money for the rest of your life, which becomes costly. For this reason, many people are skeptical about using a Financial Advisor.

Should You Use a Financial Advisor?

The choice of whether to use a financial advisor, in the form of a broker, a CFP, or an Investment Advisor, is more of a personal one rather than a general one. In other words, you must look at your circumstances and see if it fits your budget, time, and unique investment strategy. One of the things that you need to consider is the kind of investments you are making and how risky they are. Generally, the more risk you are willing to take on, the more you should be ready to use the services of a financial advisor. For example, if you are investing in mutual funds, there is little need for a financial advisor. However, you want to enter the stock market to purchase individual stocks. In that case, the risks you are taking are more significant, and you should employ the services of a professional to assist you in managing the portfolio.

Another point to consider is the size of your portfolio. The larger your portfolio is, the more likely you will need professional advice. Plus, a broader portfolio account can easily absorb the fees of hiring a financial advisor.

Finally, it would be best if you researched before using a financial advisor. One of the best ways to get a financial advisor is to ask people around you who have enjoyed success in the stock market over a consistent period. While past profits do not guarantee future earnings, it is easier to trust someone with a record of being somewhat successful than someone without much success in the market.

If possible, create a list of as many advisors you'd like to speak to and schedule a conversation with them. It would help if you did that offline, by the way. While online interviews and conversations are good starters, you should not trust a person or company with your hard-earned money without meeting them. When you meet, ask questions about their investment strategy, whose trading style and philosophy they subscribe to, and how they plan to manage your portfolio. Most of the time, the first consultation is free, as it allows you to get to know each other without the pressure of finances forcing you to perform. The other thing is, as this is free, you can meet several and choose one whose mentality suits yours.

When you meet, ensure you do not leave the meeting with doubts about what you're getting into. Do not allow yourself to be deceived with high-sounding and complex language you do not understand. It would help if you insisted that every term you do not understand and every service charge is explained. Of course, you must be fair in your dealings too. Your advisor is a professional and deserves to be paid well for their expertise and sometimes experience.

Digital Alternatives to Financial Advisors

Recently, more brokerage companies have been implementing digital investment management solutions. Two of these new developments are robot- advisors and Online Financial Planning services.

A robot advisor is a digital service that offers simplified and low-cost investment management. To make use of it, you answer a few questions on the brokerage company's website, and then complex algorithms help you build an investment portfolio according to the goals you have set and the risk appetite you have indicated that you are comfortable with. In this way, robot advisors help monitor and balance your investment, ensuring your portfolio is managed correctly. What's more, a robot advisor costs a fraction of what a real-life human financial advisor will cost.

Another option is online financial planning services. This is more like a traditional advisor than a robot advisor. The online service gives you access to human financial advisors who can help you manage your investments, among other things. Some packages grant access to the type of automated investments you'll get from a robot advisor and the ability to consult with a team of financial advice-. Some more expensive alternatives grant you access to the one-on-one service you will receive from a traditional offline advisor.

Surprisingly, both options are relatively cheap, as well as being flexible. Some companies even charge a large percentage of their fees from the profits they help you make. Before you select a financial advisor, primarily online, ensure that you understand everything they offer and possibly speak to their support teams to understand what exactly you will be charged.

Mutual Funds

A mutual fund is a financial vehicle that is made of a pool of money that has been collected from many investors. These funds are then used to invest in assets and securities such as bonds, stocks, instruments in the money market, and other types of investments. A professional money manager manages the portfolio of a mutual fund. They collate the funds' assets and invest them in a diversified portfolio to produce gains for the investors. The objective of a mutual fund is to generate income for the investors. The mutual fund's prospectus states that the portfolio is structured and maintained to match the investment goals.

Investing in a mutual fund gives individual investors such as yourself access to a professionally managed and diversified portfolio of bonds, equities, stocks, and other securities. Every shareholder will gain and lose proportionally to the gains and losses the funds make. Mutual funds tend to invest in many shields, and the fund's overall performance is tracked as a change in the fund's market capitalization, which is an aggregated performance of the individual investments in the portfolio.

Understanding Mutual Funds in Depth

A mutual fund works by aggregating money from multiple investors to build an extensive portfolio, then investing that money in various types of assets. These include bonds, securities, and equities. Thus, the overall value of the mutual fund depends on how each security or investment is performed. So, in purchasing a mutual fund unit, you are buying into the mutual fund's performance or, better still, a part of the portfolio's value. You have invested your money into buying a fraction of many types of assets - a condition that you could not. Have carried were you to support on your own. This makes a mutual fund different from other types of stock investments. A share in a mutual fund represents a share in many different stocks and other assets.

For this reason, the price of a share of a mutual fund is called the Net Asset Value (NAV) per share, sometimes referred to as the NAPS. A mutual fund's NAV is found by dividing the total value of all the securities it holds by the total number of outstanding shares. Outstanding shares are held by all institutional investors, shareholders, insiders, and company officers. Also, the value of a mutual fund's claim can be bought or redeemed at the current NAV, which remains stable, unlike the stock price. The NAV of a mutual fund does not fluctuate but is settled at the end of each trading day.

Income is earned from a mutual fund in 3 significant ways. Interest is made on the dividends in stocks and interest on bonds held in the portfolio of the funds. Generally, a fund pays out most of the funds it receives in a Single year to investors through a distribution. Usually, there is an option for investors to either receive a check or reinvest the earnings to get more shares.

If the fund sells assets that have been appreciated, then the fund is said to have a capital gain. Most funds also transfer these gains to the investors during a distribution at the end of a financial year.

If the fund holdings appreciate but are not sold by the fund manager, the fund shares increase in price, and then you can sell your mutual fund shares on the open market.

Should you invest in a mutual fund?

Why should you consider investing in a mutual fund? For starters, mutual funds help eliminate or at least reduce risk. As we have said in a previous chapter, diversification is essential to keep your chances low. Or put in simple language, you shouldn't put all your eggs in one basket. Consider an investor that invests in Apple or Amazon stocks. The investor would lose money if the buy came before the company had a lousy quarter because all his investment is tied to that company.

On the other hand, somebody will mitigate if the investor uses that money to buy shares in a mutual fund. That is because the mutual fund has stocks in other companies; the loss will count for a small part of the fund's portfolio. In this way, a mutual fund helps you avoid any significant losses, but at the same time, you don't get any big wins either.

Imagine the flip side of our analogy, where Amazon or Apple had a great quarter and outperformed the competition. Any investor investing solely in that company would have made much money. On the other hand, an investor in a mutual fund with a stake in a company will not make as much profit because that company's stocks are only a part of the fund's portfolio. It's a classic risk and reward scenario: the higher your risk, the higher your chances of reward, and vice versa.

It is essential to say that if you are already investing in a retirement package, you are most likely investing in some mutual fund. In this case, you can decide to go for a riskier alternative. You might decide to invest directly in the stocks of a company.

So, as a recap, let us re-examine what we've looked at in this chapter. While you can invest in the stock market on your own, sometimes, it may make sense to look at hiring the services of a professional financial advisor. However, the fees charged by many traditional professional advisors are high and can hurt your portfolio, especially if it isn't ample. A good alternative is a robot advisor or an online financial planning system. These digital platforms provide financial services like traditional financial advisors but usually at a much cheaper rate. They consider your present financial situation and goals and help you plan how to achieve them. Lastly, you can invest in a mutual fund if you are seeking a way to diversify your investment and reduce risk. However, you should know that your profit might tend to be on the low end. Remember, again, high risk, high reward, and low risk, low reward.

CHAPTER FIVE

How The Best Of All Time Invest (And What History Shows Us)

They say if you want to be successful at anything, learn from those who are already successful. Thus, in this chapter, we'll look at some of the greatest investors and how they invested. We'll look at trading strategies and how to select the one that is best for you.

But first, what is an investment strategy, and what types do we have?

What is an Investment Strategy?

If your plan to invest in the long term can be likened to a football match, your investment portfolio is your game plan. The right investment strategy can and will increase your chances of success. To achieve financial freedom, you need to have a solid plan for managing your investments. I advise that you have an investment strategy before placing your first trade. It's the second thing you need to learn how to do immediately after you know what a stock quote is and how to buy it.

Why is it Important to Define Your Strategy?

The right investment strategy is like having an instruction manual to guide you through the investment process. It will help you identify and pick the suitable investments for you and your goals and avoid investments that look promising but will perform poorly over time.

When creating an investment strategy, you must precisely determine your goals. A proper investment strategy starts with a concrete plan you are trying to achieve. For example, a goal like "to be financially independent" or 'to be able to retire early,' while being a good and noble goal, is unrealistic and cannot help you make concrete and realistic progress. Instead, you should set a goal: "I want to achieve an annual return rate of 7% on my investment contributions over the next 15 years, to amass $600,000, that I can retire on." The more specific your goals are, the easier it is to decide how exactly to make progress toward achieving the goals. This is doubly important if you are not hiring an investment manager. This means that you must be meticulous about investing your money. There are many investment strategies; the real work is finding the one that fits your goals and circumstances. The golden key to success is to pair the right plan with the right goals.

In addition to the right goals, you need to represent your current financial situation accurately. How much does it cost you to live? What are your monthly expenses? How much debt are you in? Can you handle debt? What are your spending habits, and how often do you save? Often, investment fails in the long term because of consistency and good management. It would help to consider the impact that investment will have on your finances so that you don't get into trouble halfway. If you can afford it, you can speak to a CFP to help create a plan. While you do not need to have them on retainer, their expertise can help you when you start investing.

The next thing you need to decide is what your risk tolerance is. I've spoken extensively throughout this book about risk and risk tolerance. Risk tolerance talks about how much risk you will expose your investment to. For example, putting all your assets on a single stock is quite risky because a fall in the price of that stock will mean that all your investment loses value, and a rise will mean that all your investments will increase in value. Some factors should consider your risk tolerance, such as age, income, and how long you have until you retire. Generally, the younger you are, the more risk you can take because you have more time to recoup any losses.

Let's look at some of the greatest investors and their investment strategies.

Benjamin Graham's Investment Philosophy

When it comes to investment philosophies, one person that is worth looking at is Benjamin Graham. He is known as the father of value investing, an investment style many modern-day investors adopt. But first, let's look at who Benjamin Graham was and how he got to Wall Street.

Early Years

Benjamin Graham was born in London in 1894 but moved to New York as an infant with his family. Graham was a gifted academician and won a scholarship to Columbia University and eventually graduating second in his class. His family lost their savings in the Bank Panic of 1907. He joined Wall Street due to the financial pressures of his family, as his father had died, and he needed to become the family breadwinner. He turned down a teaching position at Columbia University and took an entry-level job at Newburger, Hender, and Loeb. Graham had risen through the ranks within a few years. He moved from runner to clerk, to market letter writer, to analyst, and finally became a partner at age 26.

He left Newburger in 1923 to start his firm and partnered with Jerry Newman to launch Graham- Newman.

How his Trading Style was built

In the early days of Benjamin Graham, he set the foundation for building a systematic method of fundamental analysis, one of the methods of analyzing a company. During this period, the rest of Wall Street depended on rumors and insider tips to make large profits. However, Graham sought mate information about any company wherever he could before making decisions.

Before the SEC was created in the 1930s, company information was scarce. Only insiders in a company and moguls on Wall Street had access to this information. However, the average investor was left in the dark. With the resources available, Graham could search for and find many pieces of relevant information, thus gaining an edge in the market.

For example, one of Graham's first big waves as an investor was on a popularly called "Northern Pipeline Affair." Northern Pipeline was one of the companies spun off from Standard Oil when they were ordered to break up by the court. As a fellow on Wall Street, he discovered this company was trading at a discount to a portfolio of liquid securities and cash. The shares were trading at

$65 a share, while the cash share and high-grade bonds were worth $90 a share. Graham then took a position and attempted to convince management to distribute the investment portfolio to shareholders. Management and shareholders were, however, not convinced. When He failed to win the board over, he took more decisive action, fighting by proxy for two seats on the board. After winning both seats, the commission agreed to distribute the excess capital.

Value Investing and Books

The crash of the stock market in 1929 caused Graham to lose almost all of the investments that he had made and subsequently taught him critical things about the stock market. His observations throughout the crash and as he rebuilt drove him to publish a book called *Security Analysis* with his former student David Dodd. Another great American investor, Irving Kahn, contributed to the book's content.

The book was published in the early days of the Great Depression in 1934 when Graham lectured at the Columbia Business School. This book taught the basics of the Value Investment strategy. This strategy involves buying stocks that are currently undervalued and have enormous growth potential as time goes on. It is important to note that at this time, people viewed the stock market as a speculative vehicle, and the idea of an intrinsic safety margin or value was first espoused by the book *Security Analysis*. The concept of fundamental analysis is a system where the business or company itself is studied, rather than the market, was espoused by the book.

As taught by Dodd and Graham, the idea behind a value investment strategy is to derive the stock's intrinsic value without considering the current market price. Investors can determine a stock's intrinsic value by considering company factors like earnings, assets, and dividends. If it is determined that the stock's intrinsic value is much higher than the current price, then the buyer should purchase shares in that company and hold them till there is a mean reversion. The mean reversion is an idea that as time passes, the intrinsic and market price will move closer and converge at a price that reflects the stock's actual value. This would occur if the market were efficient, a theory that Graham believed in. If the market is efficient, a company's intrinsic value will eventually be reflected by the change in market price.

Graham also believed in a margin of safety provided for by investors' irrationality, such as their lack of ability to predict the future and market variations. This, Graham argues, is certain to deliver a safety margin or space for human error that the investor can invest in.

Let's take an example of how this method works. If you were an investor considering purchasing stocks in a company X. The company is well-known and is a leader in its industry. The stores are trading at

$100 per share; meanwhile, it earns $10 per year as a profit. Meanwhile, a competing company Y is a younger company that is not as well-known but earns less, at $2 per year. The stock is also valued at $15 per year, which is much cheaper.

Using Benjamin Graham's method of investing, somebody will use these, and other figures will be used to perform a fundamental analysis of the company. In this case, company Y is cheaper than company X to buy every dollar of earnings. The Price to earnings ratio (we covered this in Chapter 2) for company X is 10, while for company Y is 7.5. Using Benjamin Graham's method of investing, you will conclude that the stocks of Company X are over-priced because of their popularity. As such, the investor will be better served to choose to invest in buying the stocks in Company Y.

In 1949, Graham wrote the widely acclaimed book. *The Intelligent Investor: The Definitive Book on Value Investing.* This book is widely considered the bible of value investing and features a character known as Mr. Market, a metaphor for market price mechanics. Mr. Market is the imaginary business partner who tries to sell shares to or buy shares from the investor. Mr. Market is ofttimes irrational and shows up at the investor's doorstep with varying prices depending on how optimistic or pessimistic he feels today. This is an analogy of the irrationality of the market. Of course, the investor is not obligated to accept any offer at any time. Graham's point is that instead of relying on daily market sentiments, which.

If run on the greed and fear of investors, an investor should analyze how much a company's stock is worth based on the company's reports of its operations and financial position. According to Graham, the intelligent investor sells to optimists and buys from pessimists.

In another chapter, we cover value investing in more detail, but I want you to be familiar with this philosophy. Successful investors, such as Warren Buffet, a literal student of Graham in his classes at Columbia University and a student of Graham's investing methods, adopted this same philosophy. **Warren Buffet's Investment Philosophy**

Warren Buffet is the most well-known investor of the 20th and

21st centuries. He has consistently maintained a high ranking on Forbes' list of billionaires. His investment strategy has reached mythical heights; many other brokers and investors claim to follow it. Warren Buffet follows some necessary tents and an investment philosophy that is now extremely popular and widely followed around the globe.

Brief Background

Buffet formed the Buffet Partnership Ltd. In 1956, less than ten years later, by 1965, it was in control of Berkshire Hathaway. By June 2006, he announced his plans to donate his entire fortune to charity.

Investment Philosophy

Warren Buffet's investment philosophy is heavily influenced by the thoughts espoused by Benjamin Graham, with Buffet credited with saying, "I'm 85% Benjamin Graham". Like Benjamin, Buffet's investing style involves finding undervalued and average companies and diversifying his investment portfolio through them. His investment philosophy might look, but it is complex.

First, Warren Buffet only restricts himself to investing in businesses he understands and can analyze successfully. He considers an in-depth understanding of how a company operates to be a viable forecast of how the business will perform.

As we said, value investing involves looking for and finding currently underpriced stocks. As such, they expect their values to rise as the intrinsic value and market price converge. Buffet, however, takes this to another level. He isn't concerned with the supply and demand intricacies of the stock market. He isn't worried about the stock market's activities at all. His famous quote demonstrates this mentality: "In the short term, the market is a popularity contest, and in the long term, it is a weighing machine."

Therefore, his philosophy is to choose stocks based on the company's overall potential. Selecting and holding stocks is a long-term play. The Buffet isn't seeking capital gain in this investment philosophy, but ownership in quality companies can generate earnings. Thus, when Buffet invests in a company, he isn't so much bothered about whether the market will recognize its worth; instead, he's more concerned about how well that company can make money as a business, which makes all the difference.

Warren Buffet's Methodology

To select companies that are valuable but under- priced, he asks some crucial questions about himself and the company. A direct relationship exists between the stock price and its level of excellence. Warren Buffet understands this, and he carefully examines this relationship. Of course, apart from this, different factors need to be analyzed too. This relationship is merely one of the criteria you must remember while selecting stocks or a company to invest in.

Company's Performance: The return on equity or ROE often measures a company's performance. It is also known as the stockholder's return on investment. It primarily showcases the rate at which the investors earn income on their shares. By comparing one company's ROE with other companies, Warren Buffet usually determines how well a company performs within a given Industry. The net income divided by shareholder's equity provides the return on equity. Before deciding to analyze the company's performance history, Buffet will carefully go through the ROE of a given company for the previous 5-10 years.

Level of Debt: Another ratio commonly used to measure whether a company's value will increase in the future is the debt-to-equity ratio. The portion of the debt is always supposed to be relatively lower than the equity present in the company. Only when the level of debt is trimmed will the earnings generated from the shareholder's equity increase. A higher level of debt shows that the company needs to perform better. Divide a company's total liabilities by the shareholder's equity to calculate the debt-to-equity ratio. This ratio gives a bird's eye view of the proportion of funds used by a company for financing its assets. If this ratio is high, then it means that the company is relying on debt to finance its purchases. A high debt-to-equity ratio generates earnings volatility and higher expenses incurred toward interest payments.

Profit Margin: You can calculate the company's margin by dividing the net income by the net sales. The simplest way to determine a company's profitability is by looking at its profit margin. A reasonable profit margin combined with the scope for increasing the profit margin shows that the company is highly profitable. Usually, a seasoned investor like Warren Buffet will check the profit margins for the previous 5 or 10 years. A high-profit margin and an increase in this margin show that the company is adept at managing its finances and optimally utilizing its funds.

Company Status: Buffet usually opts for companies that have been around for at least ten years. This criterion effectively eliminates all those companies which have had their IPO (Initial Public Offering) within the last decade. He created this system because it helps him invest only in companies he thoroughly understands. He seldom invests in the newer tech companies coming up these days. Value investing is based on investing in undervalued companies that have been around for a while so that their track record can be carefully analyzed. It is one factor you must consider, and don't solely rely on a company's track record while investing.

Reliance of Commodities: Warren Buffet only invests in a business whose products are unique from its competitors. Apart from this, he also avoids investing in companies that don't offer anything special. If the product offered by a company is not unique, it means that others can easily replace it. Only when a need has a competitive advantage will it be able to increase its value in the future. Or it has to offer something the competitors need help duplicating quickly.

Costs Involved: This brings us to Buffet's final factor while finalizing an investment. Finding a company meeting all the criteria mentioned above might be relatively easy. However, it might be challenging to find one which not only satisfies all the conditions discussed up until now while still being undervalued. Determining the company's intrinsic value and analyzing the business fundamentals are quintessential at this stage. This is trickier than merely calculating the liquidation value if somebody sold the company today. However, it excludes certain intangibles, such as the brand name and identity. Once the company's intrinsic value has been determined, it is compared to the current market capitalization, which is the current total worth of the company. If the inherent value measured is 25% higher than the market cap, then the company is viewed as valuable and can be invested in.

As simple as this sounds, the entire process depends on how accurately you can judge the company.

Peter Lynch's Investment Philosophy

Another of the most successful and well-known investors of all time, he came into the limelight in the late '90s and early 2000s. He was appointed a portfolio manager of the Fidelity Magellan mutual fund in May 1977. Incidentally, this was his first job as a portfolio manager, and he succeeded in growing the asset fund from $20 million to the biggest mutual fund in the world. Moreover, he consistently outperformed the market by a whopping 13.4% annually. The most significant part of all this is that Peter Lynch achieved this by using basic principles that he is happy to share with anyone that cares to listen to. Lynch firmly believes that individual investors have an inherent advantage over larger firms because they can't or won't invest in smaller-cap companies that haven't received considerable attention from analysts and mutual funds. He detailed his strategy in his best-selling book "One Up on Wall Street," written in 1989, and another in 1994 named "*Beating the Street.*"

Peter Lynch's investment is somewhat like that of Warren Buffet and can be summed into 3 points,

Only Buy What You Understand: According to Lynch, our eyes, ears, and common sense are the most excellent stock market research tools we possess. Lynch was proud that his most significant stock market ideas were discovered while strolling in the grocery store or casually chatting with family and friends. He believes we can all perform first-hand analysis as we take in information from the world around us; it merely depends on how we process it. While traveling, driving, reading the dailies, or any other mundane tasks, you can as well discover new investment opportunities. If consumers represent two-thirds of the United States GDP, it means that most of the businesses on the stock market are in business to serve an individual customer. Thus, if something about a company attracts you as a consumer, you should consider paying more attention to it to invest. **Do Your Research Thoroughly:** Picking a company you are attracted to, and love is one thing, but you must do a thorough and comprehensive research before investing. Do not confuse the seeming simplicity of the philosophy to mean that research does not play a significant role in the success Lynch recorded. Lynch highlights some fundamental values when selecting stocks you want to invest in.

Percentage of Sales: If a product or service attracted you to a company, then you should check what percentage of sales that product makes to be meaningful. A great product or service that doesn't make more than 5 to 10% of the company's total sales will have minimal, if any, impact on the company's bottom line.

PEG Ratio: Peter Lynch is credited with inventing the Price-to-Earnings Growth ratio. It is the valuation ratio to the rate at which the company's earnings are growing. This ratio tells you how much expectation is built into the stock, and as such, you want to invest in companies with a healthy growth rate of earnings and reasonable valuations. A company with a steady growth rate with a PEG ratio of two or more already has the earnings growth built into the stock price already, leaving little to no room for error.

Select Companies that have strong cash positions and debt-to-equity ratios that are below average. Companies with stable cash flows and assets that are prudently managed to give the company options in all market environments.

Invest for the long term: Lynch firmly believes in investing in the long-term game. He said that "absent of many surprises, stocks have been relatively predictably stable for the last 10 – 20 years. You might as well flip a coin to decide whether they'll be higher in the next two or three years". While this kind of speech from someone on Wall Street might seem surprising, it shows how much he believed in his philosophy. Lynch conducted a study with unexpected results. The study was to determine whether timing the market was an effective strategy to jump on.

According to the strategy's results, if an investor had invested $1,000 per year on the day stocks were at their absolute high for that year for 30 years, ranging from 1965 – 1995, that investor would have earned a compounded return of 10,6%. Meanwhile, if another investor invests $1,000 every year for the same 30 years on the day the stocks were at their lowest for the year, this investor will have earned 11.7% compound interest. In other words, after 30 years of investing at the worst possible time, the first investor trailed the second by a mere 1.1% per year. This is why Lynch believes that trying to predict the direction the market will move quickly is not worth the effort. Somebody will better spend that time researching a picking a strong company. If the company is strong, the stocks will appreciate as the business makes more money.

In conclusion, there is a seeming emphasis on picking and investing in the best and healthiest companies; better put, the greats favor a strategy about precision. In other words, you must work to do the research and find out how dependable and profitable the company is likely to be in the future.

CHAPTER FIVE

Active Investing Strategies

Now we have examined how to choose an investment strategy, as well. We will discuss some of the investment strategies famous and successful investors have used in this chapter and the following active and passive investment strategies.

What are Active Investment Strategies?

Active investment strategies are just that, strategies that require your active participation. It would help if you did loads of research, pay attention to the company's financials, etc. It is quite tasking, to be honest, but the rewards are lucrative. If you select a good enough company, you can hit it big. For example, if you invested in Netflix. As far back as 2003, when a share was spilled adjusted for less than $5, your stake will have risen to $40 in 2004, a meteoric rise of 700% in less than a year. Of course, you might not always make the right call, but with stocks like this, you might only need one to recoup all your losses. Before discussing this further, let's look at Fundamental analysis and why it is crucial for active investing strategies.

Fundamental Analysis

Fundamental analysis is one of the ways of viewing the business at a basic financial level. This sort of analysis looks at the critical ratios of the company to decipher how healthy the business is, financially speaking. Fundamental research also shows you what common stock's value should be like. Several components are considered: revenue, earnings, the business's cost, interest rates, and asset management.

Many speculators utilize Fundamental Analysis in isolation, but it may be helpful to combine it with other tools to value the stocks before deciding to invest—the objective of using Fundamental. The analysis is to figure out the stock's present worth and, more importantly, how to stock is valued by the market.

Should you not be planning to do the fundamental analysis by yourself, understanding the terms and key ratios used to evaluate a company will allow you to follow a company's stock carefully and decipher which will be the best to invest in.

It's About the Earnings

Fundamental analysis and investment portfolios are all about profit. Investors want to be aware of the profit the company is making right now and the future profit potential. It might be complex to calculate; however, the most important thing about choosing a stock to invest in and determining a rising stock price often indicates a regular dividend. If the earnings do not meet the projected cost, it can bring down the price of the shares. Businesses report the profits made each quarter. As such, analysts use these reports to examine the company's health and then raise the alarm when the companies do not make expected earnings.

Tools used for fundamental analysis.

As significant as earnings may be, they usually only show you something meaningful with another input source. Revenues alone do not entirely capture how the market values a stock. You will need additional fundamental analysis tools to construct a perfect image of how the market loves the store.

Some Ratios that You Need to Know

While we've covered most of the ratios you should know in Chapter 3, we'll review a few important ones again for fundamental analysis.

Most of these ratios are not that hard to find out, and what's more, you can see most of these ratios already calculated on many financial websites like MSN MoneyCentral or CNN Money. In any case, if you ever need to calculate them yourself, you should note that the essential tools for Fundamental Analysis depend on growth, market value, and profit. Here are the ratios that are important for you to learn:

Earnings Per Share (EPS): Each stock reflects the amount of the company's profit. EPS calculated as the net income on the selected shares is then divided by the available shares.

Price to Earnings Ratio (P/E): The P/E ratio compares the stock's selling price to the company's earnings per share.

Projected Earnings Growth (PEG): This ratio anticipates the rate at which the stock earnings grow.

Price to Sales Ratio (P/S): The P/S ratio shows the value of a company's stock compared to the revenue. It is also known as Revenue, sales multiple, or PSR.

The dividend payout ratio is obtained by comparing the dividends paid to Stockholders to the company's net income. It is what accounts for payment that doesn't get paid out externally but is retained to be used for growth that is potentially possible.

Price-to-Book Ratio: This ratio is also called the price-to-equity ratio. It compares the market price of a stock to its book value. To get this, we divide the most recent closing price of the stock by the book value of each share of the last quarter; the asset's value as it is found in the books of the company is the book value. It is the asset's cost minus the cumulative depreciation.

Dividend yield: the ratio of the share price compared to the yearly dividend. It is written in percentage form. To get this, divide the dividends paid within a year by the share's value.

Return on equity (ROE): we get this by dividing the net

income by shareholders' equity. This gives us a return on equity (ROE). It can also be called the firm's return on net worth.

Remember that all the above numbers are tools, so you should not use any single number or ratio in insulation. They can't give you a suggestion to buy or sell by themselves; instead, we should use them in conjunction with other ratios. Well, you are looking for the perfect stock to invest in; all these ratios should be the benchmark used to gauge the value of that potential investment.

Value Investing

The first type of active investing strategy that we will look at is value investing. Value investors are more or fewer shoppers looking for a bargain. They seek out undervalued stocks, then buy them and expect their values to increase as time goes on. In value investing, the Investor is looking for stocks that they believe have lower prices than the intrinsic value of such security. Value investing is based on some level of irrationality in the market. It is this irrationality that value investors, in theory, seek to profit from. It presents an opportunity to buy a stock at a discounted price and wait for the value to increase.

A value investor can find a deal without combing through volumes of financial data to find a bargain. Many Mutual funds allow investors to select and invest in undervalued stocks. For instance, the Russell 1000 value index is a famous benchmark value investors use, and many mutual funds imitate this index.

The underlying mentality behind Value Investing is that you are not just buying a stock but a company. Thus, a value investor looks at more than store performance charts. Instead, more attention is paid to the company. In other words, the value investor examines the company it believes will increase in value the most over time and then invests in it.

However, value investing can be tricky because valuing a business is usually subjective. Everyone has access to the same information. The valuation that is made based on this information can vary quite widely. This is because different investors do have varying levels of risk tolerance. The company's intrinsic value is almost entirely subjective and depends on the investor's industry knowledge and personal bias. So, while you can look at the historical data, it does not necessarily guarantee a trend in the future. The real trick of value investing is to buy something that you know is currently worth less than it is, why you do not see how much it will be worth. You should remember that value investing is not just about buying undervalued stocks but buying good stocks currently undervalued. For this reason, successful value investors advise beginners to invest in Industries they are conversant with and confident in. The more you know about an industry, the more accurate your judgment about a company and its stock in that industry is likely to be.

How to Pick Profitable Stocks

Let's look at how to select good stocks to invest in. When picking stocks to invest in, you should focus more on the company than the price stocks themselves. By this, I mean that you should see yourself as a stakeholder and the company owner because that is what you are. When you buy a stock in a company that is publicly traded, purchasing a portion of the company's ownership. So, as a value investor, you should view yourself as though you were the company's sole owner. If you were to be the company's sole owner, how diligent would you be with your research? That is the attitude you want to use when doing the fundamental analysis of any company you are interested in before you decide to invest in their stocks. It would help if you remembered that bang and trading stocks are a long-term goal rather than a short-term one, usually looking at a minimum of 5 to 10 years of holding the stock. This is why you should do extensive before investing in a particular company.

When researching stocks, keep your eyes open for those that have:

High Dividend Yield: This is the percentage paid to the investors from the store compared to its price, the higher this value is, the more valuable the stock is. However, it would help if you only came here with results in the same industry to get an accurate result.

Low Price to Book Ratio: As I explained, this ratio compares the book value and market value is the better the company is. This hints at what will be left if the company gets liquidated.

A Low Price to Earnings Ratio: compare the share's price to what it will earn. The goal is to pay less for the stock and profit more.

Any real value investing is in the investing game for the long term. You must be able to look past temporary losses and see the big picture. A perfect example of this is seen in Warren Buffet. When investing in value, he does his homework on companies, sometimes analyzing them for years before purchasing a stock, but once he does, he is committed to the long-term. For example, when Warren Buffett invested quite heavily in the airline industry, she was quoted as saying that the airlines "had a bad first century" and that he hoped that they had gotten that century out of the way. The choice of the stocks to invest in properties should be based on decades of evidence of that company's performance and is also made with a decade of future performance in mind.

Value Investing Tools

Traditionally, value investing requires the Investor to perform detailed and exhaustive research. However, beginner investors may need more time or skill for that research detail. The P/E ratio has rapidly been adopted as the primary tool investors use to identify cheap or undervalued stocks quickly. As we said earlier, this number comes by dividing the share price of a stock by the earnings-per-share of the same stock. A lower P/E ratio usually means paying less than $1 of the current earnings. Therefore, value investors typically look for companies that have lesser Price-Earnings ratios.

While the Price-Earnings ratio is quite a good place to start, many experts insist that more is needed to make the strategy function as effectively as it should. The Financial Analysts Journal published the research which stated that: "strategies that involved quantitative investment based on this kind of ratio were not a good enough substitute for the strategy of value investing that make use of a more comprehensive approach to locate and identify stocks that are undervalued," According to the research, the reason many investors are usually confused and lured in by the low PE ratio stocks that are based on accounting numbers that are generally temporarily imported. Many times, caused by false high-earning figures, which is the denominator in the equation used to calculate the PE ratio. When the actual earnings are reported eventually, they are usually lower than analysts forecasted. Thus, a return to the true mean ensues. In other words, the P/E ratio increases, and the intrinsic value the investor thought to invest in suddenly vanishes.

To avoid becoming victims, the researchers advised investors to utilize quantitative approaches to detect such anomalies, such as combining values derived from the PE formula with momentum profitability and quality measures to avoid the so-called value traps.

In conclusion, value investing will work only when those investing are prepared to stick with such a company for an extended period and is also ready to put in serious efforts to research the stock. A study by Dodge and Cox showed that value investing strategies almost always perform better than growth.

They were investing in strategies when viewed over ten years or even more. The result of the research then showed that value investing strategies only performed worse than growth investing strategies for three 10-year periods when we view the previous 90 years as a case study. These periods were the Great Depression. Which spanned from 1929 to 1940, the bubble of the technology stock, which took place between 1989 – 1999 and the years between 2004 and 2014/15

Growth Investing

This is the second type of active investing strategy. In this strategy, they are looking for undervalued stocks, and group investors lookout for investments with the potential for solid growth in the future. An investor employing a growth investing strategy is looking for a company that will produce the following significant phenomena. However, good investing is not just some reckless method of speculative investing; instead, it is the ability to evaluate the current health of the stock and its growth potential. Successful growth investing must consider the prospect available to the company as a result of the sector that it is in. For example, you will have to think if electric vehicles have a future. Before you decide to invest in a company like Tesla, consider if artificial intelligence will soon become Commonplace before you choose to invest in a data science company. For this service or product offered by a company to grow, there needs to be evidence that somebody will widely accept such a product or service and that there is a robust appetite in the market for such a product. Growth investors answer these questions by examining the company's recent history. This is done because, in theory, a growth company's stock should be growing; that is, the organization should be able to show a trend of earnings that is strong and consistent, proving the company's ability to meet investors' growth expectations.

One of the disadvantages of group investing, however, is that there are few to no dividends. Growing companies usually need capital to maintain their expansion, meaning there will be little cash left to pay investors dividends. Moreover, growth with faster endings also comes with higher valuations, creating a much higher risk for many investors.

Is growth investing effective?

Research shows that a value investing strategy tends to perform better than a growth investing strategy when viewed in the long term; this does not mean that growth investors do not profit from their plans. A study by the Stern Business School at New

York University reported, "While growth investing underperforms value investing for long periods, there existed shorter sub-periods in which a growth investing strategy did dominate. The major challenge of growth investing is determining where such "sub-periods" will happen.

It is interesting to note that we can determine when a group strategy will likely perform better than a value investing strategy by looking at the National Gross Domestic Product, or GDP. This is seen if you look at the years 2000 - 2015 throughout this period, including strategy value strategy for seven out of the fifteen years (2007, 2008, 2009, 2011, 2013, 2014, and 2015)). The GDP growth rate was less than 2% for five of those seven years. On the other hand, a strategy based on value investing outperformed a growth strategy for nine years and seven out of these. In nine years, the Gross Domestic Product was higher than 2%. We can see that the growth investing strategy tends to be more profitable when the GDP is reduced.

Growth Vs. Value Investing

Which strategy do you use? Do you concentrate on growth or value? Which of these strategies will generate a better ROI in the long run? Historically, growth stocks tend to do better when the interest rates and GDP decrease while a company's earnings increase. On the other hand, value stocks do well when the economy is recovering but do not do so well when the market is going through a bullish phase.

All those interested in investing in the long run usually invest in a combination of value and growth stocks to mitigate the risks involved while increasing the chances of earning higher rates of return. This approach will allow an investor to earn profits in a usual market condition where somebody will recover somebody any losses made, and the returns will increase over time.

CHAPTER SEVEN

Passive Investing

So far, we have examined active investing strategies where you must do a book of research and follow up on the stocks you've purchased to ensure that you make your desired profit. However, passive investing is a good alternative for those who need more time, patience, or the required skill to do this research. Passive investing is an investment strategy that seeks to maximize the Returns investigated by minimizing buying and selling. One common passive investing strategy is index investing, where an investor purchases benchmark representation such as the S&P 500 index and holds it for a relatively long time.

Passive Investing

Passive investing generally refers to a buy-and-hold portfolio strategy aimed at a long-term investment horizon and, thus, has a minimal trading horizon in the market.

Passive investment is generally cheaper, less complex, and often produces superior results after tax when considered for medium and long-time horizons compared to actively managed portfolios.

Index Investing

This is a passive investment strategy; whose goal is to generate returns like that of a broad market index. Investors use index investing to reproduce the performance of a specific index, such as fixed income or detailed index, by buying exchange-traded funds (ETFs) that are built to track the underlying index closely. Index investing has several advantages. Research has shown that index investing tends to perform beyond and above active portfolio management when viewed over a longer time frame. Also, the hands-off approach that passive investing utilizes helps eliminate many of the biases and uncertainties that arise with an actively managed portfolio.

Understanding Passive Investing

Passive investing methods avoid the limited performances and fees of frequently making trades (buying and selling stocks). The goal of a passive investor is to build wealth gradually. Thus, passive investing is also known as a buy-and-hold strategy; they buy security and consider owning it long-term. Unlike the case of active investing, a passive investor does not seek to profit from short-term price fluctuations or changes in the market timing. The idea behind passive investing is that the market will post positive returns over a long period.

A passive investment manager will generally make you believe that it is challenging to out-think the market and requires more considerable effort; as such, they seek to match sector or market performance. Passive investment attempts to replicate the performance of the market by building a well-diversified portfolio of single stocks that will have otherwise required extensive research if done individually. Index funds were introduced in the 1970s and easily achieved returns aligned with the market. When exchange-traded funds or ETFs, which track major indices such as the SPDR S&P 500 ETF (SPY), came in the 1990s, the process was simplified further by allowing investors to trade index funds themselves as though they were stocks.

Pros and Cons of Passive Investing

A well-diversified portfolio is essential to investing successfully, and passive investing is an excellent way to achieve this diversification. Index funds, used in passive investing, spread risk by holding all or a representative sample of the securities in their target benchmarks. The goal of an index fund is to track a target benchmark or index rather than seeking stocks that are winners of buyers; hence, they avoid constantly selling or buying Securities. This helps eliminate transaction fees and operating expenses from an actively managed investment portfolio. An index fund offers investors simplicity and an easy way to invest in any closing market because it tracks an index. There is little or no need to monitor an individual manager or choose among several investment teams.

On the other hand, however, passive investing is subject to total market risk because of index funds. Track the entire market. When there's an overall fall in the stock market, or the prices of bonds fall, index funds also follow suit. Managers of index funds are generally prohibited from taking defensive measures such as reducing a position in shares, even when it looks obvious and the manager thinks that the prices of shares will fall. Index funds that are passively managed first constraints on their performance as they are naturally designed to track the benchmark index rather than attempt to perform exceptionally well.

Some of the pros of passive investing are:

- **Meager fees:** Because there is nobody selecting stocks. Oversight is much less expensive. Passive funds follow the index that they used as the benchmark.

- **Tax efficiency:** passive investing is typically tax-efficient because the strategy does not result in a substantial capital gains tax for that financial year

- **Transparency:** what assets are in an index fund?

- **Simplicity:** a group of policies or an individual index is much easier to comprehend, manage, and implement than a complex and dynamic strategy that requires consistent research and management.

A potential drawback of passive investing is that the potential returns are more diminutive. By the very definition of passive investment, even during times of market upheaval. Passive Investments might occasionally beat the market; they will rarely post the significant returns active managers seek unless there is a boom in the market itself. Active managers can, on the other hand, bring in more substantial rewards while, of course, taking on more risk. Will an extension of the same old rule, the higher the risk, the more the premium, and vice versa?

Why are Index Funds Popular?

One of the main reasons index funds are quite popular among investors is because of the immediate diversification they offer. As mentioned in the earlier chapters, diversifying investment portfolios helps mitigate the risk of loss. With a single purchase of index funds, an investor can effectively invest in stocks of different companies. For instance, whenever an investor invests in an index fund based on the S&P 500 index, the investor can access the ownership of stocks in 500 companies. This is an excellent strategy to reduce the risk of investments from a loss you might have gained had you invested in just one company. Funds like the S&P 500 index funds allow you to invest in different companies across various industries. However, certain index funds will enable you to invest only in certain sectors, countries, or even specific types of investments. This is one of the reasons why the S&P 500 index funds are amongst the most popular index fund options. Apart from diversity, their return is high, and the risks involved in trading are low. As with other stocks, fluctuations can creep in, but historically, index funds provide a consistent return of around 10% in profits annually.

Best Index Funds for 2022

Now that we've talked a bit about passive investing and index funds, it's time to look at some of the best index funds in 2022 as a guide to investing your money and starting your journey to financial freedom.

We'll look at Vanguard as they are one of the best and biggest index funds on the planet. Investing in Vanguard funds is a little complicated compared to using a simple robot Advisor. Before we go further, we must touch a little on fees. Even though I explain this in Chapter 2, you should understand the expenses involved. Don't overlook this aspect because it can cost you 1-25% of your earnings from investing. This is simply atrocious, and it gets many beginner investors to turn to index funds like Vanguard in the first place.

Even if you aren't too keen on passive investing, it is prudent to start using Personal Capital Fee Analyzer to check the fees payable on your investment account.

Also, before I go on, let's quickly establish the difference between an ETF and a mutual fund. Vanguard defined ETF as a collection of numerous stocks and bonds in a single fund, similar to an index fund. The one significant difference is that you can automate your investments using mutual funds. However, opt for an ETF if you want to reduce the amount payable as fees and aren't averse to manually making your monthly contributions. Vanguard offers mutual funds and ETFs but has different risk-reward ratios and prices. For a Vanguard ETF, you can start with as low as $1. On the other hand, the minimum initial investment can be between $1000 and $3000 while investing with Vanguard Mutual Funds.

Total Stock Market (ETF) - VTI

NYSEARCA: VTI | Vanguard | Morningstar | Fee: 0.04% | 5 Year Avg: 9.58%.

This is the Vanguard flagship fund, and it is still their best. This ETF is a Vanguard Total Stock Market Index Fund share class. It is a blend of large, medium, and small-cap companies in the US and tracks the performance of the CRSP US Total market index.

This fund has the lowest expense ratio I've ever seen because it tracks a few smaller indexes, allowing it to be mostly automated. When most people mention investing in Vanguard, they usually refer to this fund. This fund is so successful that 92% of fund managers cannot beat this.

Social Index fund (Investor Shares)

Mutual Fund from Vanguard with a Fee of 0.18% and a % year average of 10.89%

This VTI has an element of socially responsible investing applied to it. It is aimed at companies that are either environmentally sustainable or focus on the social impact of their operations and activities. These companies use renewable energy to power their activities or support equal pay for all genders. Some companies that follow these strategies are Tesla, Apple, Google, and Microsoft. Reducing the cost of energy or attracting the best of talents are suitable for the business, and as such, it is not all that surprising that this fund performs than VTI.

Vanguard Target Retirement 2050 Fund (Investor Shares) – VFIFX

Mutual Funds from Vanguard with a Fee of 0,15% and a 5-year average of 6.25%. This fund is a life-cycle type of fund. In other words, the risk tolerance and investing direction change as you, the investor, grow in age and your investment goals change. It starts with most of the portfolio invested in stocks, and then assets are gradually relocated.

As time passes, the entire point of the life-cycle fund is to take risks at a younger age and slowly reduce the risk you are under as you get closer to retirement so that market fluctuations and changes do not affect your required money.

While this could be better regarding the fees, it helps bridge a gap in most people's portfolios. The number in the fund name, such as "2050," corresponds to your regular retirement date.

SPDR S&P 500 ETF Trust (SPY)

The SPDR S&P 500 ETF started the wave of ETF investing and has been around since 1993. It is a popular investment option, even today. With over

With $262 billion in assets, it is amongst the most popular and largest ETFs available. The industry titans, State Street Global Advisors, sponsor this fund and track the S&P 500. The expense ratio is 0.09%, meaning every $10,000 invested will cost about $9 annually.

This is amongst the best S & P 500 indices available. This investing option gives investors access to owning S&P 500 stocks at a marginal cost and the benefits of diversification of investment portfolio and risk management. Because of all these benefits, it is certainly not surprising that these are believed to be the most significant funds on the market today. If you want to invest passively, these are your best options.

CHAPTER EIGHT

What Are Diversification and Asset Allocation?

When it comes to protecting your investments, diversification and asset allocation are some tactics you can use, this chapter examines diversification and asset allocation and how to use these to safeguard your Investment Portfolio from losses and increase gains.

What Is Diversification?

Diversification is a technique that helps you reduce risk by allocating your investment to various financial instruments, industries, and other categories. Diversification aims to maximize Returns By investing in different sectors or Industries that will react differently to the same market event. This way, you are not caught flat-footed or unawares by any shift or change in market conditions. Every investment manager or professional worth their salt will agree that, while diversification does not necessarily eliminate loss, it is crucial to see you reach your long-term financial goals while minimizing risk. Let's examine why that is true and how to diversify your investment portfolio.

A Brief Look at Risk

When investing, investors are usually confronted with two major types of risk. The first kind is called undiversifiable, systematic, or market risk. This kind of risk is the risk associated with every single company period, the common causes of this kind of risk at things like inflation rates, political instability, interest rates, war, and exchange rates. This kind of risk is not specific to any industry or company and cannot be eliminated or reduced by diversification. It's a risk that you must accept. The following kind of risk is called diversifiable risk; it is also known as unsystematic risk and is specific to an industry, a company, a market, a country, or an economy. Somebody can be eliminated via diversification. The most common sources are financial and business risk. As such, the idea behind diversification is to invest in various assets and asset classes such that your entire portfolio will not be affected by market events.

Reasons for Diversification

Reasons for diversification quickly become apparent when you take time to think about it, as you mean you have a portfolio that consists only of manufacturing companies. Suppose an issue affects the manufacturing industry negatively, such as the workers going on strike or a government ban or restriction. In that case, the share prices of manufacturing companies' stocks will drop, which means that your portfolio gets hit with quite a substantial loss. However, if you had invested a portion of your portfolio into another industry, say in the shipping or airline industry, then only a part of your portfolio would be affected. The value of the shares of companies in the shipping industry may increase because importation is likely to increase when manufacturing goes down. But you can diversify even further by investing in another industry that is entirely unrelated because anything that affects trade internationally could affect both stocks. Therefore, you will seek to diversify across more than just various companies or industries. The less the correlation among your assets, the better.

It is important to diversify among various asset classes. Asset classes such as stocks and bonds will not react similarly to an adverse market event. Thus, a portfolio with a combination of multiple asset classes will be less sensitive to market swings and possibly reduce the loss your portfolio will have experienced. Generally, equity and bond markets tend to move in opposite directions, so if you have a diversified portfolio across both markets, unpleasant movement in one asset class will be offset by the positive results you will gain in the other asset class. Finally, diversification should also include location. It would help to look for investment opportunities beyond your immediate geographical area. So, if you stay in the United States, for example, you should invest in assets outside the states, say in Europe or Asia.

Problems That Arise with Diversification

Diversification is, hands down, one of the best things that can happen to your investment portfolio, but it has its disadvantages too. A diversified portfolio is cumbersome, especially if you control multiple investments and holdings. Secondly, diversification affects your bottom line significantly. This is because investment vehicles come across differently. As such, buying and selling them can be expensive, from transaction fees to charges from your broker, and since higher rewards can only come with higher risk, you might end up limiting your results.

There are different kinds of diversification, and many synthetic investment products have been built to accommodate various risk tolerance levels of investors. However, many of these products are complicated to run and are meant to be used by something other than beginners or smaller investors. For a small-time investor with little substantial financial backing for hedging activities, bonds are the most popular way to diversify your portfolio.

Unfortunately, even the best analysis of a company, its stock, and your investment cannot guarantee that it will not be a losing investment, so diversification does not prevent losses; instead, it helps you reduce the impact of a loss or a negative market trend on your portfolio.

What is the Optimum Number of Stocks to Own?

Mathematical models and studies have shown that a well-maintained and diversified portfolio of between 25 and 30 stocks yields the most cost-effective level of reducing risk. Investing in securities will provide further diversification benefits but at a drastically reduced rate.

Diversification According to Asset Class

Investors and fund managers try to diversify their investments across different classes of assets and then ascertain the percentage of investment to be made in each category. The following asset classes can be used to diversify the investment portfolio.

- Shares or stocks of a publicly traded company.

- Corporate bonds and any other fixed-income debt instruments issued by the government.

- ETFs or exchange-traded funds comprise a variety of marketable securities belonging to different sectors or index commodities.

- Different real estate types include buildings, agricultural properties, livestock, land, and other natural resources like precious metals and minerals.

- Cash and other highly liquid short-term investments -

treasury bills, certificates of deposit, money market instruments, and any other low-risk investments.

Further diversification is possible in various asset classes by selecting stocks across different industries that aren't related or by choosing supplies with varying degrees of market capitalization. When it comes to bonds, then investors can opt for bonds issued by the U.S. Treasury, municipal bonds, state bonds, investment-grade corporate bonds, and so on.

An investor can increase the degree of diversification by opting for foreign securities since they are unrelated to the securities issued by the investor's country of residence. For instance, the factors affecting the U.S. economy might not be at play in a foreign country. So, the investor's foreign investments will be undisturbed even if the local stock market takes a blow.

The Retail Investor and Diversification

One of the significant constraints for sufficient diversification of a portfolio is the time and budget available to individual investors instead of traditional investors. This is one of the reasons why mutual funds are pretty enticing to retail investors. Mutual funds offer diversification of portfolios across multiple classes of assets. ETFs provide an opportunity for regular investors to access new markets like commodities. An investor with a $100,000 investment portfolio can easily invest across different types of investments across various ETFs without overlap.

Asset Allocation

Nothing Formula can provide the best way to allocate assets for every investor. However, most financial professionals know that the decision on the way to distribute your purchases is a critical one, which means that the journey of selecting the individual securities to invest in is secondary to how you allocate your assets to various asset classes such as stocks, bonds, and cash as well as their equivalent. Investors allocate their assets differently based on their objectives. An individual saving for a new car in the short-term, say, next year, might invest the cash savings in a very conservative mix of certificates of deposit, short-term Bonds, and cash.

Another individual saving for their retirement, which could be decades away, typically invests most of their money in an individual retirement account (IRA) in stocks; such a person has a longer time to withstand the market's short-term fluctuations. Risk appetite and tolerance also play a vital role in this. An individual not comfortable investing in stocks for a long time must invest cash in a more conservative asset class.

Asset Allocation Based on Age

Generally, stock investments are meant to be held for at least five years. Cash and money market accounts are much more appropriate for short-term objectives such as those less than a year—bonds for somewhere in between the short and long range. Financial advisors usually recommend subtracting the investors' age from 100 to determine what percentage of the Investment Portfolio should be in stocks. For instance, a 40-year-old should invest 60% of his portfolio in stocks. Other variants of this rule exist that advise the individual to subtract their age from 110 or 120 as life expectancy continues to grow. The idea, however, is that as individuals move closer to the retirement age, their portfolios should move towards a more conservative asset allocation to protect their accumulated assets.

Allocating assets via lifecycle funds

Asset-allocation mutual funds, which are also called lifecycle funds or target-date funds, attempt to provide investors with a portfolio structure that addresses their age, investment choices, and risk appetite asset classes in the appropriate proportions. However, this method has its critics, who point out that standardized solutions for allocating assets prove problematic as individual investors should possess unique solutions. An excellent example of this is the Vanguard target retirement 2030 fund. In 2018 the fund had a 12-year horizon until the shareholder is expected to reach their requirement age. As of 31st of January 2018, the front comprised 29% bonds and 71% stocks. As the years pass, the phone will slowly shift to a more conservative 50:50 mix, reflecting the investor's need to preserve the capital and take less risk. The fund will move even further to 67% bonds and 33% stocks in the following years.

Assets Allocation Vs. Diversification

While asset allocation and diversification are closely related, they are different. Asset allocation describes the percentage of a given portfolio held in various asset classes. Diver-satisfying and rebalancing, on the other hand, comprise allocating assets. So, asset allocation is more about the proportion of the portfolio appointed to various asset classes, and diversification is concerned with the investment itself that is invested in.

Rebalancing means changing the proportion of different assets within a portfolio. Asset allocation and fall out of alignment as the investors change their investment outlook and the economy changes. Rebalancing helps the distribution of assets within a portfolio to reflect the level of risk that the Investor is now comfortable with. Professional investors constantly seek to rebalance portfolios, while individuals rebalance less frequently.

Risk Tolerance

Risk tolerance measures the degree of uncertainty an investor will be willing to accept in exchange for higher or lesser gains. Investors with a higher level of risk tolerance will be ready to offer short-term losses in exchange for a potentially higher return. Risk tolerance also determines how much you must invest; a more extensive portfolio means you have more capital and can absorb more losses over time.

In conclusion, how you decide to allocate your acid and diversify your portfolio depends on you, your personal goals, and your age, size of portfolio, and risk tolerance. Most brokers have an education system, especially about their products, that explain how and why certain assets are allocated the way they are. If you want to diversify, ask questions from the company you are investing in, whether you are investing in mutual funds or Exchange- trust-Fund (ETF).

CHAPTER NINE

Setting Your Personal Investment Goals

Congratulations! You are almost ready to launch out. Before you do, however, you must answer some questions and build some investment goals for yourself, but how do you go about it? A quick online search for financial advice will deliver many resources and answers. It looks as though there is so much to choose from, and in this era of content marketing, every bank, broker, independent financial adviser, and their mother and looking to tell you what to do with your money.

Now, we have covered financial advisors in a separate chapter and, as such, will only go so deep into it here. The focus of this chapter is to help you build a personal investment plan that you will follow for the rest of your life. Whether you hire a professional financial advisor or not, an investment plan will help you decide your goals and objectives and spending habits that can get in the way of them.

Hire a Professional or Do it Yourself?

When it comes to investing, you can either hire the services of an investment adviser or create an investment plan by yourself. It is entirely up to you; choose accordingly. However, if you think you can get on by yourself, here are a couple of questions you must answer before coming to conclusions.

Do you like to read and learn about topics related to finance? Are you open to learning about different concepts like investment, taxes, loans, or personal finance? Knowledge is an indispensable resource, and you cannot do without it regarding investment. So, if you are naturally inclined towards learning about financial topics, your work will interest you. Your natural desire to learn will help you make better decisions and develop a sound investing strategy. Even if you don't like to read, before you start investing, it is quintessential that you do all the necessary homework. Start learning about personal finance and financial planning. Apart from all the information in this book, a wealth of knowledge is available online. After all, you are investing your hard-earned money, so learning about the different options is a good idea.

Review Your Current Financial Position. This is relatively easy if you are used to keeping track of your expenses, income, and savings. If not, you must start doing all this before considering investing. After all, you might end up overspending if you aren't sure of the funds available. You must be able to keep track of every single penny you spend. Once you do this, shift your focus toward your savings. Investing will help increase your income, but you must always have sufficient savings before investing. Start by learning to manage your finances, and only then attempt investing. If this seems too much for you, seek the help of an investment planner. How do you feel about making your own financial decisions? Have you planned for your retirement? Regardless of your earnings, you must permanently save for the future. Even if you have a

A comfortable and stable job that helps you rake in six- figures annually, you must concentrate on planning for your retirement. It is always better to save for a rainy day than be caught unawares. Also, take some time and think about whether you are comfortable handling large sums of your hard-earned money or not. If you don't feel confident about this, then hire a professional to do the necessary.

Will you handle the stock market volatility on your own? You will be your financial advisor if you want to do everything yourself. It would help to familiarize yourself with all the different investments in the stock market, learn about market trends and conditions, and develop self-control. You must know the right time to enter and exit the market. Apart from this, it would help if you learned to regulate your emotions while investing. Feelings of fear and greed can effectively burn a massive hole in your pocket if you aren't careful.

Managing your finances isn't scary; it only takes discipline, planning, saving, and investing. You can always manage your finances. You can start learning now even if you think you can't do this. After all, there is no time like now to learn about becoming a good investor and financial manager.

How to Set Investment Goals

Now, let's take some time to talk about setting investment goals. Lots of people have some idea of how they want their financial future to pan out like. Depending on where you are in life, you probably already have a dream of financial freedom. It could be sending your kids to college without needing to enter debt or being able to build your dream home. Many people, however, is that you don't know how to make your dreams become a reality, and so this section will detail how to make your financial future as accessible and secure as you can.

The first step to achieving your financial and Investment is to write them out. As simple as that may seem, it is a crucial first step to achieving your goal. The act of physically writing out your goals translates them from just a distant dream to a vision that you can see and begin to work on from now.

So briefly list out any short-term goals that you have. The keyword here is to be brief, talking about him in bullet points; a more detailed list will come later. You want to save for or purchase short-term goals within the next five years. An excellent example of a short-term plan could be replacing your car's tires or taking that vacation overseas that you've dreamed of. Next, you want to separate these goals into needs and wants. You must have a need, while a want is something you would like to have but is optional for you to have.

After that, make a brief list of your long-term goals. You want to achieve long-term goals in the next 5-years or even more. Whether to get married, have children, and your retirement can be classified as long-term goals. This is because these decisions will impact how you will live your life in the nearest future. For instance, if you are planning to get married, you should plan to move out of that two-bedroom apartment you are sharing with your roommate. Your long-term goals will be different based on your age. For those in their early 20s, things like marriage, kids, and a home fall under the classification of a long-term goal. But for another individual in his late thirties, his kids' college fund or retirement will probably be closer to a long-term plan. So, think and ask yourself what will make you happy or give you peace and fulfillment.

Once you've done that, it's time to investigate the details. List your goals in the order of most important to least important. With the most important at the top and the least important at the bottom, be as specific as possible instead of just writing your retirement as good at a particular number. Finally, attach a time frame to your goals. All reasonable goals have a time limit. For instance, if you are in your thirties and want to retire at 60, you have about 30 years to reach any retirement goal. So, do this for every plan that you have written down.

Here is an example for you to follow.

1. **Dream Home -** Build our $500,000 dream home within the next 20 years.

2. **College fund -** Save $125000 within the next 15 years for my kids' college tuition.

3. **Retirement -** I have $1000000 in my retirement fund by age 60.

Once to have a rough estimate of how much your future will cost you. It's time to take stock of how much you have. How much can you afford to set aside each month or year? When you know how much you can afford to set aside per time, it's time to build your investment portfolio. At this point, you need information, and luckily this book is full of it. Go back to Chapter 1 and start reading slowly, applying all the information in each chapter. By enquiring from brokers and financial advisers, you know how to invest your money and begin making moves.

I suggest that you sit down with a financial adviser, even if it's just for a limited time, for them to look over your plan and give you a few tips. Even if you're not planning to hire one for the long-term, and I don't think you should anyway, getting a second or even third Eye to look over your plan is for the best. So, look around for a financial advisor that is cheap and yet competent, and request a meeting with them to discuss your financial plan. You should revisit the project occasionally every few years to see where to revise.

Qualities of Investment Goals

As you set your financial and investment goals, here are a few things you want to remember. Your goals must be measurable: You must make sure that your goals are concise, clear, and definite. For example, saying that you will set a goal of saving $1000 per month is helpful because you can look at your finances and determine if you did for that month. On the other hand, a goal that says, "I will save more money each month," is useless because it does not hold you accountable and is not measurable. Your goals must be reasonable and rational: if your goal is to reach a million dollars in personal net worth by the age of 40, you have to use things like the time value of money formula to calculate whether or not the present rate at which you are saving will be sufficient, setting aside $5000 a year, as good as that may sound, will not get you there. Thus, you need to lower your expectations or increase the amount of money you're setting aside and choose an investment platform such as stocks to increase the amount you are potentially building up. Your goals must be compatible with your lifelong objectives: I cannot emphasize this enough because if you go through life with the mentality that money is the only thing that matters, you might end up rich but sad and miserable. Always remember that money exists to serve you — nothing more, nothing less. The entire purpose of having money or being financially free is to allow you to experience more happiness and utility. It makes no sense to sacrifice all your health to pursue money, for example, and then spend all your money to fix your health when you're older.

In conclusion, building a financial plan is not magic; all required is common sense, patience, and discipline. That mix is purely unbeatable.

CHAPTER TEN

Protecting Your Investment and Selling Stocks

Warren Buffet, one of the most successful investors, has a golden investment rule- never to lose money. It doesn't imply that you must sell your investments or holdings the minute they depreciate (this might be the best opportunity to purchase instead of the market). However, as a rule of thumb, stay put with your position up to the amount of loss you can withstand. All investors hope their investments are profitable, but you must first secure your capital in the long run to become a successful investor. As mentioned earlier, there are different steps you can follow to mitigate the risks while investing in the stock market. The strategies discussed in this section will help safeguard your portfolio.

Diversification

We've already treated this topic extensively in another chapter, so I will only go into some detail, but diversification is essential to protect your capital. The modern portfolio theory (MPT) believes in diversification as one of its cornerstones. A diversified portfolio is more likely to outperform one concentrated when viewed over a more extended period. According to several financial advisors, between 20 and 30 stocks eliminates almost all unsystematic risk.

It is investing in Assets that do not Correlate.

There are two types of risks that every investor will face: unsystematic risk and the opposite, systematic risk. Systematic risk is generally associated with an investment in any market. Systematic risk is the kind of risk that is inherent to every need, unfortunately. It is possible to mitigate its impact by incorporating assets that do not correlate to your portfolio or even going as far as to add asset classes that are not connected, such as currencies, real estate, commodities, as well as bonds, to the stocks that you probably already have in your investment portfolio. Assets that are not correlated react differently to market changes, sometimes even moving in opposite directions so that if an investment or an asset class goes down, the other is on its way up. This gives your portfolio a level of security and stability as compared to if your portfolio only contained stocks. Investing in assets that do not correlate helps you reduce the volatility of a portfolio. Unfortunately, using non-correlating assets does eliminate the higher and lower ends of the profit margins that could be seen if you were actively investing alone and produces returns that are more balanced, at least theoretically.

Put Options

From 1926 to 2009, the mutual fund index S&P 500 reduced in value for only 24 years out of the 84, or in other words, slightly above (25%) twenty-five percent of the period. In these situations, investors sometimes protect their gains by drawing some of their already-made profits. It may often turn out to be an intelligent choice, and often, it may not. This is because, in many instances, winning stocks may sometimes plateau for a bit before rising higher. In such cases as this, you don't want the store sold off, but at the same time, you want to cash in on some of the profit you have made, so how do you go about it?

There are several ways to do this, but the most used option is to purchase put options. A set option is like a bet on the line stock that will reduce the price. This differs from when you short the store; the put option allows you to sell the stock at a specific price at some point in the future, giving you some much-needed stability and confidence, irrespective of what the market goes through.

So, assuming you own a hundred share units of company X, the shares have risen in value by 80% in one year and are now being traded at $100 per share. As such, you are convinced that the stock price will increase in the distant future, but at the same time, you're concerned that the stock has risen far too rapidly and, as such, will likely fall in the short term. To protect your gains, you will purchase one put option of the company X, with an expiry date of 6 months ahead, sold for a strike price of $105, and could even be slightly more than that. The cost of purchasing this option will then be$6 per share or $600, which gives you the right and ability to sell 100 share units of company X at $105 sometimes before it expires in 6 months.

Should the share price fall to, say, $90, the price of buying the option will increase by quite a significant margin, and you can then sell off the opportunity to make a profit and eliminate the fall in the stock price. Investors that want to be protected in the long term can also decide to buy Long-Term Equity Anticipation Securities (LEAPS), which usually come with much more extended periods, sometimes up to 3 years.

Stop Losses

A stop-loss order can help protect your investment from the falling prices of shares. There are various kinds of stop-losses that you can use. A hard stop will trigger a sale on a stock once its price reaches a particular value. For instance, if you purchase company X's Shares at $10 for a share, using an order for a hard stop set at $9, then the stock automatically is sold off If the price hits $9. Trailing stops, however, is quite different in that it tends to move alongside the stock price and could be pre-set to either percentage or dollars. Maintaining the example above, as you mean, you set the trailing stop to 10%. Should the stock increase by $2, the set trailing stop order moves from $10.80 to $9.

Should the stock price later fall till it gets to $10.50, with the hard stop set at $9, you still retain ownership of the stock. However, somebody will have sold off the share for $10.80 with a trailing finish. Whatever follows this, however, determines which will have been more profitable. A trailing stop loss would have been more advantageous if the stock price had dropped from $10.50 to $9. However, if the price had later moved to $15, you would have been better off with a hard stop loss.

Critics of the complex and trailing stops claim that it makes temporary losses permanent, while the proponents of the orders believe that it helps protect you from markets that change rapidly. I will advise, however, that somebody must plan well, and any stop you use must be very well prepared.

Dividends

Investing in dividend stocks is a strange way to safeguard your portfolio. Historically, rewards are responsible for a significant portion of the total return. In many instances, a store brings even the total amount.

One of the proven methods for providing returns that are higher than average is by owning stable firms that pay out dividends. Also added to the income invested, studies have shown that the companies which pay their investors more significant rewards tend to increase their earnings at a faster rate when compared to those that do. More rapid growth will often lead to share prices rising higher, which will, in turn, generate even more capital gains.

But how exactly does this help in protecting the portfolio? It does this by basically increasing the overall return. As the prices of stocks fall, the cushion provided by dividends is considered necessary for investors that are averse to risks and will usually result in low volatility.

So, while providing a cushion when the market is in a downturn, dividends are also excellent protection against the effects of inflation. Via investments made in blue-chip companies, companies that have pricing power and pay dividends, you give your portfolio the kind of protection that other investments with fixed income cannot match, except for TIPS or (Treasury Inflation-Protected Securities). What's more, if you do invest in companies that have had their dividends increase consecutively for the past 25 years, called "dividend aristocrats," you can say for sure that such companies will increase the amount they pay out each year while the pay-out of bonds remains roughly at the same level. As you get closer to retirement, you want to prepare to prevent increased inflation from destroying your money's purchasing power.

Notes Protected by the Principal

Investors concerned with maintaining their principal should look at notes protected by the principal and have equity participation rights. They are like bonds in that they are securities with fixed incomes that return the principal investments to the investor if it is held to maturity. However, the significant difference is that equity participation is simultaneous with the guaranteed principal.

For example, if you considered buying $1,000 worth of principal-protected notes fixed to the S&P 500. This note will mature in 5 years, and the party issuing them will then purchase zero-coupon bonds, which will grow roughly the same period that the letters will have discounted to Face value. As such, the bonds wouldn't receive any interest until maturity, when you can redeem them at their face value. In the example above, the $1,000 that is in zero-coupon bonds can be bought for

$800, and as such, the $200 left can be invested into call options of the S&P 500.

These bonds will then mature and depend on the participation rate; the profits will be distributed when they reach maturity. Assuming the index increased by 20% over the stipulated period and the participation rate is 90%, you'd get your original $1,000 investment plus a profit of $180. You are essentially letting go of $20 in profits in exchange for a guarantee that your principal is guaranteed. However, if the index did lose 20% over the five years, you'd still receive the original $1,000 you invested. If you had invested directly into the index, your investment would have lost $200.

Investors that tolerate few risks will find principal-protected notes quite essential. However, before you decide to invest in it, you should take time to determine how strong the bank is offering a guarantee on your principal, as well as the notes' underlying investment of the letters and the fees associated with buying them.

How to Sell Your Stocks

Here are a couple of ways that you could use to sell a stock, with some additional background on how to decide to sell.

Order an Order

The easiest way to sell any stock is via a sell order. The primary type of orders related to sales are market orders (which involves selling the stock instantly at the market price), as well as limit order (which set a minimum accepted sales price), as well as a stop order (that initiates the sale of the stock once it reaches a sufficiently low price)

Using an App

Beginner traders are fond of trying to play the market because many investment applications do not require a commission to sell.

Using a Financial Advisor

If you purchased your stock from a financial advisor, you could also decide to sell off the stocks similarly. A financial advisor usually takes 24 hours to execute a request to sell. You should, however, note that if you make this decision, you have to talk to the advisor directly or send a written appeal. As was stated in Investopedia, "Financial institutions will not readily accept a request via email or voicemail as somebody can miss them quickly or even third parties can manipulate.

A Magic Selling Number: 16.5

This digit has nothing to do with the share price, calendar date, or secret code from a smoke-filled room on Wall Street. Instead, it pertains to something known as a GAAP forward multiple. Let's break that jargon: GAAP is "generally accepted accounting principles," a financial standard that public companies use.

If you take the earnings per share of a company as determined by GAAP and multiply it by 16.5, you now have a target price for your sale. So, if Carlozo Motors has earnings per share of $10, your target sell price will be $160.50. Why the number 16.5? This is based on a 40-year average for equities and has been in the ballpark of 16.5 since the late 1800s.

Market Timing and its Untimeliness

Someone must answer besides knowing how somebody can sell a stock. How do you decide when to sell a stock? Well, there are different answers to this question. Let us look at the various solutions starting with a technique not usually favored while selling stocks - market timing.

The concept of market timing is based on the theory that an investor can successfully buy and sell stocks by predicting the future movements of a market. This is based on guesswork, starting with the mortgage interest rates and then betting on the ideal time to sell and the price. This technique isn't precise. Most stock market experts believe this technique is a wager. Even if the world of investing is chock-a-block with numbers, there is no specific calculation to determine the ideal time to enter or exit a position. This might pay off if you don't mind taking a gamble. After all, you are effectively guessing the ideal time to get in and out of the market.

It is always better to set a specific dollar value whenever you want to sell instead of hoping to get the time right. It is like a sell order, the only difference being that this isn't a legally binding agreement. For instance, if the dollar value for sale is

$30, then if a $25 stock reaches the said price, it is time to sell. It is a better way to deal than relying on guesswork.

Putting Everything Together

Considering the various methods you can use to buy or sell a stock, entry barriers are low in the investment world. Suppose you are concerned about how to sell a stock or when you can adopt the "*sitting and waiting*" approach. The buy-and-hold strategy is one that successful investors such as Warren Buffet have used in the past.

Afterword

We've come a long way, and I want to believe that. You know all you need about stocks and the stock market to begin making money from it. We've covered quite a bit of things that are important for you to know. Somebody created for beginners who wanted to invest in the stock market had the desire to invest in the stock market but had no idea how to go about it, and I want to believe that right now, you know enough to begin investing in the stock market.

Let's quickly recap everything we've covered in this book and how you can and should apply it to profit from the stock market.

We started by looking at investments and what they are, and why you should think about creating a financial and investment plan for yourself.

We also talked extensively about risk tolerance and Investment Portfolios. In the introductory chapter, I introduced the concept of high-risk, high-reward, and low-risk low-reward. You should consider this concept as your stock market investment journey progresses.

Next, I explained the stock market and how you can make money from trading in the stock market. Then we considered a few of the greatest investors to show you what was possible via stock market trading. We also looked at the wonders of compound interest and how it can seemingly magically provide you with a fortune if you invest long enough.

In this book, I explained in depth everything that you need to know to be successful on the stock market, starting from why you should invest in the stock market to the basic fundamental knowledge you will need to understand the time to understand common terminologies that you will find as you go on things like price-to-earnings ratios, Sales ratio, book value and many more.

I also touched on practical things you will need to know to invest in the stock market, such as brokers, especially online brokers, the minimum amount you will need to open an account, and how to deal with commissions and fees, which is extremely important as it has the potential to wipe out your account if you're not careful for example in 1% commission can potentially take 25% of your Investment Portfolio if you are running an active investing strategy.

Next, we covered financial advisors as part of the strategies you should put in place to manage your money; I explained the different kinds of advice we have, such as a financial planner and investment advisor, and the fact that advisors are expensive and not the best idea for a beginner or small-time investor.

From there, I explained the alternatives to financial advisers, such as robot advisors. Finally, I ended that chapter by discussing mutual funds and why you should pay attention to them. Mutual funds offer a safe, low-risk option for a short time and beginner investors to invest and build their investment portfolio. Why diversify your portfolio and eliminate the chances of your investment portfolio losing value over the long term?

We then took an honest view of how some of the greatest investors ever made remarkable gains. We examined their trading strategies and philosophies, and in the following few chapters, we discussed the plan in-depth and the reasoning behind them. The last three branches of the book are all about index investing and why you should consider making it a part of an Investment Portfolio by looking at diversification and asset allocation to safeguard your investments. Then we ended with a look at how to preserve your investment and how to sell the stocks.

As I promised earlier, investing in the stock market is not a get-rich-quick scheme; it is a platform to generate profits via long-term investing, and that is the best way to make sustainable profits for the long term. I hope you build your investment portfolio and a future of true financial freedom by reading this book. It may be worthwhile going back through the book and taking notes to be confident that you are following the advice given. I hope you find investing in the stock market as profitable and enjoyable as I have.

Resources

1. A Review of Warren Buffett's Investing Strategy. (2019). Retrieved 31 October 2019, from. https://www.investopedia.com/investing/warren- Buffett's-investing-style-reviewed/

2. Benjamin Method. (2019). Retrieved 31 October 2019, from https://www.investopedia.com/terms/b/benjamin-method.asp

3. Coombes, A., & Jackson, A. (2019). What Is a Financial Advisor and How to Choose One - NerdWallet. Retrieved 31 October 2019, from https://www.nerdwallet.com/blog/investing/how-to-choose-a-financial-advisor/

4. Growth vs. value investing? It would be best if you considered both approaches. (2019). Retrieved 31 October 2019, from https://www.merrilledge.com/article/growth- vs-value-investing-two-approaches-to-stocks

5. Guide to financial adviser fees. (2019). Retrieved 31 October 2019, from

https://www.moneyadviceservice.org.uk/en/articles/guide- to-financial-adviser-fees

6. Maria, S. (1997). The Peter Lynch Approach. Retrieved 31 October 2019, from https://web.csulb.edu/~pammerma/fin382/screener/lynch.h

7. Pick Stocks Like Peter Lynch. (2019). Retrieved 31 October 2019, from https://www.investopedia.com/articles/stocks/06/peterlync

8. Royal, J. (2019). 5 Best Index Funds In October 2019 | Bankrate. Retrieved 31 October 2019, from https://www.bankrate.com/investing/best- index-funds/

9. The Importance Of Diversification. (2019). Retrieved 31 October 2019, from https://www.investopedia.com/investing/importance-diversification/

10. Value Investing: Stock and Strategies – Wall Street Survivor. (2019). Retrieved 31 October 2019, from https://www.wallstreetsurvivor.com/investing- ideas/value-investing/

11. What Is Passive Investing? (2019). Retrieved 31 October 2019, from https://www.investopedia.com/terms/p/passiveinvesting

Thank You

You could have picked from hundreds of other books, but you bought mine, and I appreciate it. Thank you so much for purchasing my book.

Not that you enjoyed (I hope) my book, can I ask you for a tiny favor? Can you please post a review on the platform? You posting a review is the best way to support the work of independent authors like me.

Your feedback will help me keep writing the books that will help you get the desired results. It means a lot to me to hear from you.

I am happy for anyone to reach out to me for help, comments, collaboration ideas, or feedback at brian@brianscottfitzgerald.com

My **Author page** on Amazon at

https://www.amazon.com/author/brianscottfitzgerald

www.ingramcontent.com/pod-product-compliance
Lightning Source LLC
LaVergne TN
LVHW100323210926
848480LV00003B/1239